# South Africa

# South Africa

*Revised Edition*

BY ETTAGALE BLAUER
AND JASON LAURÉ

*Enchantment of the World*
*Second Series*

Children's Press®

*A Division of Scholastic Inc.*

NEW YORK   TORONTO   LONDON   AUCKLAND   SYDNEY
MEXICO CITY   NEW DELHI   HONG KONG
DANBURY, CONNECTICUT

**Frontispiece:** A king protea plant in flower, Cape Province, South Africa.

*Consultant:* Michael R. Mahoney, Assistant Professor of History, Yale University, New Haven, Connecticut

*Please note: All statistics are as up-to-date as possible at the time of publication.*

Book production by Herman Adler Design

Library of Congress Cataloging-in-Publication Data

Blauer, Ettagale.
  South Africa, revised edition / by Ettagale Blauer and Jason Lauré.— Rev. ed.
      p. cm. — (Enchantment of the world. Second series)
  Includes bibliographical references and index.
  ISBN 0-516-24853-7
  1. South Africa—Juvenile literature. I. Lauré, Jason. II. Title. III. Series.
  DT1719.B58 2006
  968—dc22                                                          2005005704

# South Africa

# Contents

**Cover photo:**
Simon's Bay, the
Cape of Good Hope

Table Mountain

Xhosa woman

# The Struggle Continues

In 1994, South Africa held its first democratic, multiracial elections. For the first time, the black majority in the country was able to choose its own leaders. Nelson Mandela, a man who had struggled for his own freedom and the freedom of his country, was chosen to be president.

It was an amazing moment in South Africa's history. For fifty years, whites in South Africa had claimed that only they had the right, and the duty, to rule the nation even though they were in the minority. The government, which was dominated by the all-white National Party, denied most South Africans even basic rights. The government had put people in different categories based upon their race, then decided where those people could live, work, and go to school and what subjects they studied. Most people did not have the right to vote for their own leaders. In South Africa, this system of deciding people's fate based upon their race was called apartheid.

Before becoming president of South Africa, Nelson Mandela had been in prison for twenty-seven years. What was his crime? He wanted equal rights for all

*Opposite:* **A Xhosa girl in the Lesedi Cultural Village, Johannesburg**

**Nelson Mandela celebrates at the Rainbow Concert for Peace and Democracy.**

South Africans. He had joined an organization called the African National Congress and fought to gain those rights.

### The Enormous Size of the Problem

The 1994 elections marked the first time that all adults in South Africa—no matter what their color—voted for their leaders. The elections were at the center of the swift and historic changes taking place in South Africa. But they were just the beginning of a long, hard journey for the nation. Black South Africans now had equality under the law, but true equality would take much longer to achieve.

**Black South Africans wait in line to cast their votes in an election.**

**A slum near Cape Town**

The system of apartheid—a word that means "separateness" in the Afrikaans language—had divided the school system and society. Black people, people of Asian descent, and those of mixed-race heritage had been kept apart by law. They had been told that they did not have the right to live in the same neighborhood as people of other races. They were not allowed to use the same trains, bathrooms, or schools as white people. Many black adults were not prepared to take part in a modern economy. Most had never seen a computer or even an office. They had been trained to be laborers and servants.

Apartheid had created two different societies in the same country. One was well-off, well educated, and healthy. This society controlled the economy and made the laws. Its people lived in houses with running water and electricity. The other society was poor, badly educated, and without proper health care facilities. This society—most of the population—had no say in how it was governed. Many South Africans lived in shacks and had no access to clean water or electricity.

After the 1994 elections, the nation faced an enormous job. It had to bridge the gap between those two societies. Under apartheid, blacks were not supposed to live in South Africa's

President Thabo Mbeki, South Africa's second black president since the end of apartheid, was sworn in for a second term on April 27, 2004.

cities; they were reserved for white people. When the laws changed, black people flocked to the cities looking for work. But there wasn't nearly enough housing for the hundreds of thousands of people who wanted a better life. Instead, they wound up building shacks. They created enormous slums near the cities. These slums have grown into cities of their own.

Today, South Africa faces many challenges. It must try to improve the lives of the people who suffered for so long under apartheid. It must also try to create a more balanced economy that serves the entire nation.

### Democracy in Action

Despite South Africa's many problems, it has managed the change to a democratic system of government without falling into war or chaos. Unlike many countries in Africa, South Africa holds elections that are considered free and fair. Nelson Mandela announced at the beginning of his term in office that he would not run for a second term even though the law allowed it. He knew that the nation needed to experience a peaceful transition from one elected president to another.

In 1999, Thabo Mbeki became the second democratically elected president, and in 2004, he was reelected. The nation, about as old as a teenager, has shown remarkable maturity and growth in a very short time. When his second term is over

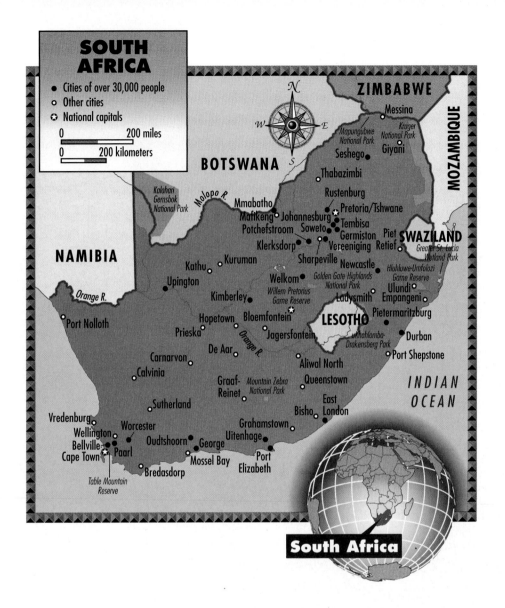

in 2009, Mbeki will leave office and someone else will be elected to take his place. While this is simply accepted practice in other democratic countries, it's an extraordinary accomplishment here. South Africa is now the country that others look to as an example of how to achieve tremendous change peacefully.

# The Look of the Land

THE REPUBLIC OF SOUTH AFRICA IS A LAND OF DRAMATIC beauty. The country is surrounded on three sides by rugged coastlines. These are formed by the Atlantic Ocean to the west and the Indian Ocean to the east and south. On some parts of the coast, strong waves crash against rocks and cliffs; in other parts, beautiful beaches spread out for miles.

South Africa stretches across the entire width of the southern end of Africa. The Cape of Good Hope, a narrow strip of land that juts out into the Atlantic Ocean in southwestern

*Opposite:* **Cat's tails bloom in the South African wilderness.**

**Chapmans Peak Drive near Cape Town**

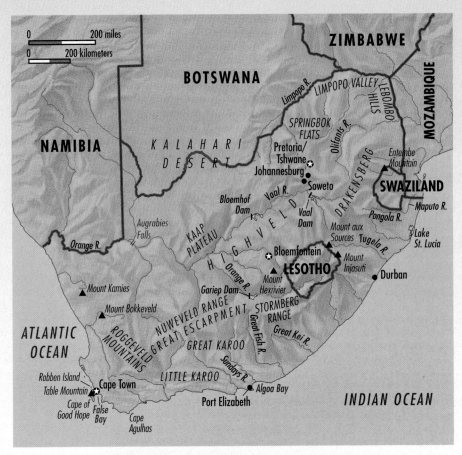

## South Africa's Geographical Features

**Area:** 472,281 square miles (1,223,201 sq km)

**Highest Elevation:** Mount Injasuti 11,181 feet (3,408 m)

**Lowest Elevation:** Sea level

**Longest River:** Orange River, 1,300 miles (2,100 km)

**Largest City:** Johannesburg

**Most Southerly Point:** Cape Agulhas

**Length of Coastline:** 1,739 miles (2,798 km)

**Average High Temperature (Cape Town):**
January 80°F (27°C); July 63°F (17°C)

**Average Annual Rainfall:** 18 inches (46.4 cm)

South Africa, has long been considered the tip of the country. But Cape Agulhas is actually farther south. It is there that the cold Atlantic Ocean waters merge with the warm Indian Ocean currents.

An aerial view of Cape Town and Lion's Head mountain

South Africa's coastline runs for 1,739 miles (2,798 kilometers). Despite this long shoreline, the country has few natural harbors. The currents and winds that sweep the oceans around the country often make traveling by ship a deadly undertaking.

South Africa shares borders with six nations. One small country, Lesotho, is completely surrounded by South Africa. To the north of South Africa are Botswana and Zimbabwe. To the northwest is Namibia. Most of South Africa's northeastern border is shared with Mozambique. Tiny Swaziland is also in the northeast.

## A Land of Contrasts

South Africa is a land of great contrasts. It includes regions of extreme dryness, tremendous rainfall, and fierce winds. In South Africa, mountains run from north to south, 50 to 200 miles (80 to 321 km) inland all along the coasts. Sometimes these mountains march right up to the sea. At the eastern end

**South Africa's Drakensberg Mountains**

of South Africa is the Drakensberg mountain range, the highest in southern Africa. The name means "Dragon Mountains" in Afrikaans. Between these massive peaks are dramatic valleys where sparkling streams make their way downhill. The earliest people to live here left behind thousands of cave paintings. The San people painted scenes of hunting and dances. Some of these paintings are still visible in this region.

Much of the center of the country is a high, dry plateau where little rain falls. Few people live in this region. In the southwest, between the mountains and the plateau, lies a smaller plateau called the Great Karoo. *Karoo* means "a great thirstland" in the language of the San. The Great Karoo is home to a few small groups and to farmers who need vast lands to graze their sheep. In the northwest, near the borders with Botswana and Namibia, are portions of the Namib and Kalahari deserts.

## Table Mountain Reserve

Table Mountain is a massive mountain that forms a natural background for the port city of Cape Town. It rises 3,563 feet (1,086 meters) above sea level and then ends abruptly with a flat top. The mountain dominates the Cape of Good Hope peninsula and can be seen up to 100 miles (160 km) out at sea. When weather conditions are just right, beautiful white clouds form over the top of the mountain, spill down its face, and then evaporate. This cloud is called the tablecloth on Table Mountain.

Thanks to the moisture provided by the tablecloth, Table Mountain has its own distinct zone of plants and flowers. More than 1,470 species of plants are found on the mountain. Many wild animals used to roam its cliffs, but now only goats and small, furry creatures called rock hyraxes are found scampering over the rocks.

A cable car runs to the top of Table Mountain. During the cable car ride, all of Cape Town and the harbor come into view. From the top, visitors can see Robben Island, 7 miles (11 km) offshore. Nelson Mandela was imprisoned there for eighteen of the twenty-seven years he spent in jail. Robben Island takes its name from the Dutch word for seals, which once were the island's only residents.

South Africa's western coastline, which stretches northward all the way to the Namibian border, is an eerie place. There icy winds blowing off the Atlantic Ocean meet hot desert air. The currents are dangerous, and many ships have crashed onto the shore. The waves pound away until little is left of the boats. Because of the many shipwreck remains, the area is called the Skeleton Coast. This desolate region often seems lifeless. But every spring, the land blossoms with wildflowers. For a few weeks, the earth is carpeted in blazing color.

## Climate

The climate in South Africa is generally warm and dry. In the winter, the temperature rarely falls below freezing. In the summer months—December, January, and February—the temperature in the drier regions may rise above 104°F (40°C).

Rainfall varies across the vast nation. In the extreme northwest part of the country, there is virtually no rain at all. The heaviest rainfall occurs along the eastern coastline. As much as 6 feet (180 centimeters) of rain may be recorded in one year in this region.

**Lamberts Bay in the Western Cape**

## Looking at South Africa's Cities

The city of Durban (below) is South Africa's largest port and third-largest city. Durban, which has a subtropical climate, is a popular beach resort. Although it can be uncomfortably hot and humid in the summer, Durban has warm and pleasant winters that make it a magnet for people from Johannesburg and Pretoria. The city was founded in 1835 on the site of the old Port Natal and was named for Sir Benjamin D'Urban, a British general and governor of the Cape Colony.

Durban is a blend of cultures. More than a third of the one million South Africans of Indian descent live in the area. The population has changed since the end of apartheid. The Zulus, once restricted to black townships outside the city, have flooded into the central district. Both groups outnumber whites, who once dominated the city.

Johannesburg (right) is South Africa's largest city and its business center. It sits on a plateau more than

1 mile (1.6 km) above sea level. The Zulus call it Egoli, "the place of gold," because it was built on top of the gold mines that gave South Africa its great wealth.

Central Johannesburg is a mix of modern skyscrapers and apartment buildings. As many as six million people live in and around Johannesburg, including an estimated two million who live in Soweto, South Africa's largest black township. North of the city are suburbs where once only well-to-do whites lived. Now wealthy blacks have also moved in.

Although apartheid has ended, most blacks still live in small houses in the townships, often without running water. But people flooding into the city live in far worse conditions. They build shacks on any open piece of land they can find. Every day, about one thousand more people arrive at the edge of the city. This shifting population has changed Johannesburg from a primarily white city into a bustling African city. Because of the vast number of unemployed people, crime is rising. Many businesses have moved out of the inner city to the northern suburbs.

So many businesses have left the inner city that the government moved its own offices in to fill up the empty buildings. Today, government offices fill the Carlton Centre, once a fashionable hotel and shopping center.

# Wild and Wonderful

W ITH A WIDE VARIETY OF CLIMATE AND TERRAIN, SOUTH Africa is home to a dazzling number of plants and animals. Many of them are unique to the country. There are more than three hundred different kinds of mammals, including black rhinoceroses, many types of giraffes, zebras, baboons, cheetahs, elephants, hyenas, leopards, lions, oryxes, and wildebeests. Once upon a time, these animals could be found throughout most of the country; today, they are found only in wildlife reserves. Population growth and hunting have eliminated the wildlife in the rest of the country.

*Opposite:* **A lioness in South Africa**

**Elephants in the Addo Elephant National Park**

South Africa is also home to more than five hundred bird species, including the African hoopoe, the lilac-breasted roller, and the crowned crane. Snakes are found throughout South Africa, especially in areas where they can hide in the grass. Most of them are not harmful to people and will slither away as soon as they sense someone coming. But one of the most dangerous snakes is the Cape cobra. If it strikes, its venom can quickly paralyze a person, leading to death.

**A Cape cobra makes a threat display in an arid region of South Africa.**

### The National Flower

South Africa's national flower, the king protea, can be found across much of the southern part of the country. Proteas have a dramatic look. A circle of spiky petals grow around the flower head, which can be as large as 1 foot (30 cm) across.

## Wildlife of the Deep

South Africa is the only country where you can see the biggest land mammals and the biggest sea mammals. Whales can be seen during the migrating season, from May to November, all along the southern coast from Cape Town to Durban.

A southern right whale breeches off the coast of Gaansbai.

The southern right whale is the main species found here. These creatures migrate all the way from Antarctica to the warm waters off South Africa to give birth and nurse their young. Humpback whales are also found in great numbers along the coast. One of the best whale-viewing places is along the cliffs of Hermanus. This town has

Jackass penguins wander the shore in Boulders.

a "whale crier" who tells visitors where the whales have been spotted each day.

Smaller sea creatures are found at a town called Boulders. Here, jackass penguins, which are unique to South Africa, come onshore and walk around the boulders that give the town its name.

## Watching Wildlife

To see most of South Africa's big creatures, tourists have to visit wildlife reserves. The best-known and largest wildlife reserves are in the eastern part of the country. The parks are carefully controlled and managed. Visitors drive along paved roads in their own cars. It's illegal to go off the road and drive over the land to look for animals. This careful control has made South Africa one of the most successful countries at protecting wildlife. If not for these efforts, creatures such as the rhinoceros would be closer to extinction.

Imagine a wildlife park the area of New Jersey—a park that's 40 miles (60 km) wide and 200 miles (321 km) long. That's Kruger National Park. Visitors to this vast area travel through fourteen different ecological areas, from forests to plains. Each area is home to different species of wildlife. Kruger is home to thirteen thousand elephants and fifteen hundred lions, along with giraffes, hippopotamuses, zebras, and more than a hundred other types of mammals.

Excellent conservation work is also done on a smaller scale. Hluhluwe-Umfolozi (pronounced "shloo-SHLOO-way oom-fuh-LOW-zee") Game Reserve is a tiny park in KwaZulu-Natal. The reserve was once the hunting ground of Shaka, the Zulu king. Today, it is the best place in the world to see white rhinoceroses, which the reserve saved from extinction.

**A grazing rhinoceros**

## New Game Parks

Most South African game parks are in the eastern part of the country, but the new Aquila Private Game Reserve is less than two hours' drive from Cape Town in the west. The park was created by Searl Derman, who is widely known in South Africa both for his charitable activities and his experience with wildlife. Recently, six Barbary lions were introduced to the reserve. This breed of lion is believed to be the closest relative of the black-maned Cape lion that roamed freely in the Cape Town area until the late 1880s. Guides drive visitors through the park in safari vehicles. Besides lions, visitors will see rhinoceroses, giraffes, and large mixed herds of springbok, zebra, wildebeest, ostrich, and many other species.

### The Springbok

The springbok is a small antelope unique to South Africa. Its ability to leap far and high made it a perfect choice as the symbol of South Africa's sports teams. To be a springbok champion means you have reached the highest level in your sport.

When apartheid ended, some people thought the symbol of the country should be changed because the springbok was associated with the old South Africa. Then, at the 1995 Rugby World Cup final in South Africa, President Nelson Mandela wore a green springbok jersey while congratulating the winning South African team captain. The crowd went wild. It was official: The springbok symbol was here to stay.

Farmers in the traditional wildlife area in the eastern part
of the country have decided to get into the game park business, too. Some of them have stopped planting corn or raising
cattle and are introducing wildlife. In some cases, the land is
actually more suited to wildlife because it is quite dry. At least
140 private preserves have been established in KwaZulu-Natal
province.

A great new wildlife park and conservation area that
opened in 2004 crosses the borders of South Africa, Botswana,
and Zimbabwe and allows wildlife the largest possible grazing and hunting area. The park in South Africa is called
Mapungubwe National Park and includes the site of a vast
kingdom that thrived more than one thousand years ago.

## World Heritage Sites

Mapungubwe is one of seven sites in South Africa that have been named World Heritage Sites by the United Nations Educational, Scientific, and Cultural Organization (UNESCO). These are places of unusual and irreplaceable importance to the world that need to be protected.

Greater St. Lucia Wetland Park (above) was named a World Heritage Site in 1999. It was put on the list because of its exceptional variety of species and for its coral reefs and coastal dunes. That same year, UNESCO also added fossil sites in the Sterkfontein Caves area, where the remains of the earliest human beings have been found. These fossils trace human ancestors back 3.5 million years.

The uKhahlamba-Drakensberg Park was named a World Heritage Site because of its caves, which are covered with paintings made by the San people. The Vredefort Dome, the world's largest meteorite impact site, was added to the list of sites in 2005.

A World Heritage Site can also be a place of political importance. Robben Island (below), where Nelson Mandela was held prisoner for many years, is a World Heritage Site.

In 2004, a natural region in the southern part of South Africa became a World Heritage Site. The Cape Floral Region is remarkably rich in plant life. Nearly 20 percent of all of Africa's plant species can be found in this small area.

# South Africa Becomes a Nation

San paintings of walking figures, San Caves

Human life began on the continent of Africa. The fossils of humanlike creatures dating back three million years have been found in South Africa. Fossils of *Homo sapiens*—the modern human species—have been found in caves in the eastern part of the country, in the region now called KwaZulu-Natal. Some of these fossils are one hundred thousand years old.

The first people in South Africa were hunter-gatherers. They hunted animals and gathered food from plants to survive. We know how they lived because the San people left paintings in caves and on rocks. The San have been living in Africa for about thirty thousand years. Small groups of San still live in South Africa today.

*Opposite:* **A man in Soweto holds up a newspaper announcing the release of Nelson Mandela.**

South Africa Becomes a Nation **33**

**The San people continue to live in South Africa today.**

About two thousand years ago, the Khoikhoi people moved into southern Africa from farther north. They settled in groups, raising sheep and cattle.

Around A.D. 300, another group of people settled in what is now eastern South Africa. These people, who were taller and had darker skin than the San and Khoikhoi, spoke Bantu languages. They settled down and raised crops and livestock. In time, the Bantu became skilled at mining and working with metals such as copper, iron, and gold. These metals became important trade goods. Most of today's black South Africans are descended from these Bantu people.

## The Europeans Arrive

Europeans first came to South Africa in 1488 when the Portuguese explorer Bartolomeu Dias visited the southern coast. The first white settlement came in 1652 with the arrival of a ship belonging to the Dutch East India Company. Its captain, Jan van Riebeeck, had been sent from Holland to establish a food supply stop for the company's ships as they made their way around the Cape of Good Hope. The garden his men established can still be seen in Cape Town, in back of the Houses of Parliament, although now only flowers are grown there.

Portuguese explorer Bartolomeu Dias arrives on Africa's southern coast.

The region where the Dutch landed was populated by Khoikhoi people. Close contact between the whites and Africans was inevitable. Most of the Dutch men had come without wives, and they sought out the women they found in the Cape. The result was mixed-race children, known in South Africa as Coloureds. They are considered a distinct race, separate from both black and white.

Shortly after they arrived, the Dutch were joined by Huguenots, Protestants who had left France to find religious freedom. German settlers also soon arrived in the Cape. Together, these three European

**Dutch Settlement**

Area settled by the Dutch in 1652

Additional area by 1700

Additional area by 1710

Present-day boundary

Additional area by 1750

Additional area by 1798

San  Native group

• Settlement

groups began to create a new language that would be known as Afrikaans. They called themselves Afrikaners, "people of Africa." They were also known as Boers, the Dutch word for "farmers."

Van Riebeeck and his men traded with the Khoikhoi and San people, exchanging metal products and tobacco for cattle, sheep, and goats. He had a fort built to protect his men and his own family. Africans from other parts of the continent and Asians were brought to the area as slaves because the Khoikhoi would not do the hard labor demanded by the Dutch. When some of Van Riebeeck's men left the company to set up their own forts, they were given land used by the Khoikhoi. For the first time, native people in South Africa became trespassers in their own land.

### The White Population Grows

Van Riebeeck had created a society in which race was the dominant feature. As the white population at the Cape grew, the settlement began to spread into the interior. The Boers wanted to be left on their own. They didn't want anyone telling them how to live or how to treat the black and Coloured workers on their farms.

In the late 1770s, as the Boers trekked farther inland and to the east, they encountered the Xhosa people. The Xhosa and other Africans lived in communities and were ruled by traditional chiefs. Many battles took place between the Boers and the Xhosa.

In the meantime, Cape Town had grown into a busy seaport, an appealing target for other Europeans. The British, who were eager to protect their trade routes, set sail for the Cape. In 1795, the British took over the Cape community from the Dutch.

**Cape Town in the late 1700s**

## Shaka Leads the Zulus

By the beginning of the 1800s, the Zulu people were living in the part of South Africa near the Indian Ocean. In 1815, Shaka came to power as chief of his people. He quickly built up his army to a force of two thousand highly disciplined warriors. Shaka was a brilliant military man. He devised a new method of fighting with a short, stabbing spear called an *assegai*.

At the same time, he arranged his armies into formations that surrounded the enemy.

Using these two techniques, Shaka and his men defeated other kingdoms. The Zulu kingdom grew into the largest in all of southern Africa. Shaka ruled for just thirteen years, but his influence on South Africa is still felt in Zululand. The Zulus are proud of their warrior history.

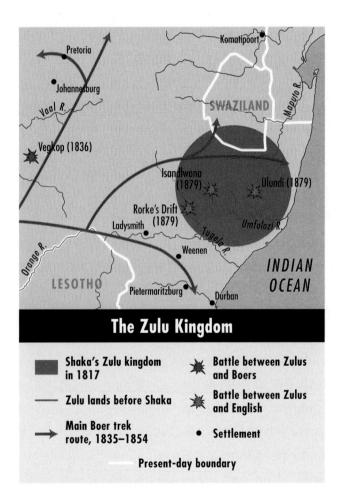

### The Zulu Kingdom

- Shaka's Zulu kingdom in 1817
- Zulu lands before Shaka
- Main Boer trek route, 1835–1854
- Present-day boundary
- Battle between Zulus and Boers
- Battle between Zulus and English
- Settlement

The first British arrivals were followed by a larger group known as the 1820 Settlers, who formed the base of the English-speaking population. The British and Dutch continued to fight over differences in language and culture. Meanwhile, the Boers were fighting the black African kingdoms. These kingdoms were also fighting each other. All of these groups were seeking land and the right to rule over that land.

### The Great Trek

In the 1830s, a group of Boers decided to trek far away from the Cape. They hated being ruled by the British. The last straw came on December 1, 1834, when the British outlawed slavery. To get away from these laws, they loaded their goods onto ox-drawn wagons and trekked over the Drakensberg Mountains.

This Great Trek brought them to lands where Bantu-speaking people lived. The Boers also met up with the Zulus, who were fierce and determined fighters. The Boers and the Zulus fought many battles dur-ing the early 1800s. The Boers ultimately won. This was the beginning of the white conquest of the eastern half of South Africa. Once the British were also in the area, the whites managed to take most of the Africans' land—and certainly the best of it.

About twelve thousand Boers traveled across southern Africa in the Great Trek.

## Conflict over Land and Minerals

The Afrikaners established their own independent states in the eastern half of South Africa. Ultimately, these became the South African Republic and the Orange Free State. This land turned out to hold much of South Africa's greatest mineral wealth. Diamonds were discovered in 1867, near the Orange River. This area was claimed by both the Boers and the British.

## Cecil Rhodes

Cecil Rhodes had a goal. He wanted the British to control all of Africa and to build a railroad to run the length of the continent. He also had a knack for making money. His drive would change the history of South Africa and the world.

In 1870, Rhodes left England for South Africa. The following year, he began buying up small mining claims in the diamond mining town of Kimberley. Rhodes and a partner then formed De Beers Consolidated Mines. It was named for the De Beers farm, one of the first places where diamonds were found. Within twenty years, Rhodes controlled most of South Africa's diamond mining industry and had an important stake in gold mining.

Soon gold was also discovered. Gold and diamonds would shape the future of South Africa. They made a few men very rich and turned hundreds of thousands of others into migrant workers. The Africans who lived on land near the new mining claims were pushed off that land in both legal and illegal ways.

The British were used to conquering people of color who they thought were not intelligent or civilized. Now they set out to conquer a group of whites who they also thought were not civilized. The British looked upon the Boers as poor farmers who were keeping them from a fortune in gold. Tensions continued to rise, and in 1899 war broke out.

The Anglo-Boer War raged on and off until 1902. By the time it was over, the British had brought in 448,000 soldiers, five times the number of Afrikaners who fought. Black Africans took advantage of the war to reclaim some of their land. But this success would not last long.

## Concentration Camps

The Anglo-Boer War touched everyone. While Afrikaner men fought on the battlefield, the British rounded up about 116,000 Afrikaner women and children and herded them into concentration camps.

About 115,000 Africans also were put into camps to keep them from helping the Boers. Conditions were terrible. At least 14,000 blacks and 28,000 whites died of disease and starvation in the camps.

Although the British conquered the Afrikaners, they agreed to many of their demands. The British agreed to recognize the Afrikaans language. They also ensured that lands were once again put in the hands of whites. The British also agreed to the Afrikaner demand that blacks be denied the vote.

### The Union of South Africa

Great Britain now controlled all of southern Africa. In 1910, the various colonies were united to form the Union of South Africa. Blacks were not given full citizenship in the union, and they did not have the right to vote. In response, they created their own organization, the African National Congress (ANC).

In 1913, the Natives' Land Act was passed. It divided South Africa into "white" areas and "black" areas, with most of the land set aside for the small white population. The cities of the new union were declared "white." Only blacks with jobs could enter the cities. Most blacks were confined to crowded black townships outside the city limits. In 1936, land distribution was finalized: whites had given themselves 87 percent of the land. Blacks, who outnumbered whites seven to

German Southwest Africa
Walvis Bay (Cape Colony)
Bechuanaland (Britain)
Southern Rhodesia (Britain)
Portuguese East Africa
Pretoria
Johannesburg
Swaziland (Britain)
Vaal R.
Orange R.
Bloemfontein
Pietermaritzburg
ATLANTIC OCEAN
Orange R.
Durban
Basutoland (Britain)
INDIAN OCEAN
Cape Town

**Union of South Africa, 1910**

- Cape Colony
- Natal
- Orange Free State
- South African Republic (Transvaal)
- Other British territory

one, were left with 13 percent of the land. Their land was the least useful and the worst for growing crops.

White farmers had been evicting black tenants since the Great Trek. But now, with the land act, most of the nation was made homeless.

### Apartheid Laws Enacted

In 1948, the Afrikaners' party, called the National Party, won the national election. The new government enacted a series of laws that became known as apartheid. This was the policy of absolute segregation of the races. It said where a black person could live, go to school, get medical care, and work. Blacks had to carry passes to prove they had jobs and the legal right to be in a city or a township.

The white-ruled government was headed by Prime Minister Hendrik Verwoerd, who held power from 1958 until he was killed in 1966. Verwoerd was notorious for two policies. One was the creation of ten "homelands," semi-independent regions where blacks were supposed to go when not working for whites. Black South Africans were assigned to one of these homelands. Blacks without jobs, even temporarily, were supposed

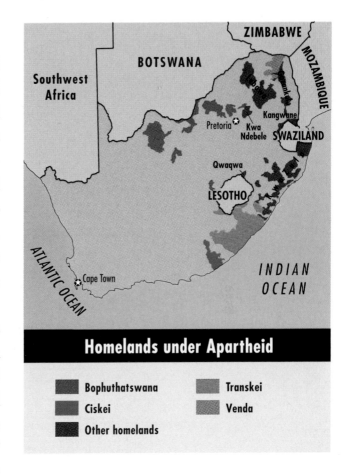

**Homelands under Apartheid**

- Bophuthatswana
- Ciskei
- Other homelands
- Transkei
- Venda

**Prime Minister
Hendrik Verwoerd**

to go "home" to a homeland, even if they had never been there before. Verwoerd claimed that black Africans were not South Africans at all, but were citizens of these homelands. Verwoerd himself had been born in Holland.

Verwoerd's other notorious apartheid policy was "Bantu education." Verwoerd believed black Africans did not need the same kind of education as white people. Bantu education limited the kind of schooling black Africans received. They were not considered smart enough to learn technical subjects. Instead, they were limited to the kind of schooling that would allow them to work as laborers and maids.

### The ANC and the PAC

The African National Congress (ANC) and another group called the Pan Africanist Congress (PAC) organized resistance to apartheid's laws. As demonstrations grew in strength, the government became determined to stamp out all protest. On April 8, 1960, the government banned the ANC and the PAC. It was now a crime to be a member of these organizations.

The tide of resentment grew as the National Party government moved to strictly enforce the apartheid laws. The government forced millions of blacks to move from their homes to fulfill the policy of racial separation. Black leaders had few choices, and all of them were dangerous. They could

## Forced Removals

Enforcing apartheid laws meant destroying the lives of black South Africans. Forced removals were among the worst things that could happen. In forced removals, people of color living in an area that the government said was "white" were thrown out of their homes. In 1955, the lively area of Sophiatown in Johannesburg was emptied of its residents. The houses, bars, and nightclubs where blacks gathered were torn down to make way for the new white area called Triomf, which means "triumph" in Afrikaans.

In 1966, the government turned its attention to District Six, in the very heart of Cape Town. District Six was close to city hall, parliament, and the city's business center. Every day, the members of Parliament saw how the people of District Six defied the whole idea of apartheid. The residents were of all races and religions, living in harmony. Most were Coloureds, but blacks and whites lived there as well.

Then the government declared District Six "white."

Shortly thereafter, soldiers came in the middle of the night and removed blacks who were living there. Neighbors woke up the next day and found empty houses and apartments where those people had lived.

Over the next fifteen years, the government forced sixty thousand people out of their homes in District Six. People and their belongings were simply tossed out on the street. Some were taken by truck to the Cape Flats—a flat, sandy area on the edge of Cape Town—where they were divided according to their race. Others were left on the sidewalk with nowhere to go and no way to get anywhere.

Once the people were gone, bulldozers moved in and reduced the houses to rubble. The plan was to build new houses for white people. But the shame of what had been done was so great that no one wanted to live there. The empty streets remained empty. No houses were built. To this day, most of the land remains vacant.

resist apartheid through organizations such as the ANC, or they could escape from South Africa and work for change from outside.

Those who fled the country are known as the exiles. They include some of the nation's most important leaders of today, including President Thabo Mbeki. The exiles slipped over borders at night and often traveled far from South Africa to win financial support and backing for their struggle. Some lived outside South Africa for nearly thirty years.

### The Sharpeville Massacre

Black South Africans tried to resist white domination, but with little success. The South African police and the army were called out every time blacks rose up against the apartheid laws that made their lives so miserable.

On March 21, 1960, a group of unarmed blacks made their way to the police station in the black township of Sharpeville. They went there to hold a peaceful protest against the passbook laws. According to these laws, no black could travel or work without a passbook. Thousands of demonstrators left their passbooks at home, expecting to be arrested. They thought this would show the government that its policy could not continue if it had to arrest

A black South African man shows his passbook.

thousands. But the peaceful demonstration was met with gun-fire. When it was over, sixty-nine blacks were dead, many shot in the back by the police as they tried to flee when the shooting began. Their deaths sparked a nationwide protest.

## Steve Biko

South Africa lurched from crisis to crisis in the years after Sharpeville. In 1968, students founded the South African Students Organization (SASO), with Steve Biko, a medical student, as president. SASO provided legal aide and medical clinics for disadvantaged black communities. Unlike the ANC, this group did not accept whites as members. They believed that only blacks could fight for their own freedom. Whites, even sympathetic whites, benefited from apartheid.

The government continued to crack down on blacks. In 1976, black students rose up in fury against a new government policy. In a country where so many different languages were spoken, one language needed to be chosen for students who reached high school. Black students wanted to be taught in English, a language in general use. The government,

**Steve Biko, South African anti-apartheid activist**

however, insisted they be taught in Afrikaans, the language of apartheid. They staged a protest march in the black township of Soweto near Johannesburg on June 16, 1976. Thousands of students boycotted classes and took to the streets.

The army was called out to put down the protest. The soldiers were ordered to fire at the crowd. A thirteen-year-old boy named Hector Pietersen was killed, and several others were wounded. Protests rippled across the country. In the next few months, more than six hundred protesters were killed. Many of them were children.

It was the start of a new era of oppression in South Africa. Young black leaders rose up to take the place of those in jail, but their efforts were stopped at every turn. Steve Biko was jailed several times and finally brutally murdered by the police while in their custody in 1977. Biko became a symbol of black resistance to his countrymen and the world.

Police and protestors clash at a demonstration in Cape Town.

**Former South African president P. W. Botha**

## Pressure from the World

The white government changed hands in 1978. The new prime minister was P. W. Botha. Botha planned to end some minor parts of apartheid, such as "whites-only" entrances to buildings and laws that prohibited marriage between whites and blacks. But these changes didn't address the real issue of equality.

Governments around the world began applying economic sanctions against South Africa. Investments in the country dried up. Corporations withdrew their businesses. South Africa found itself banned from the economic business of much of the world.

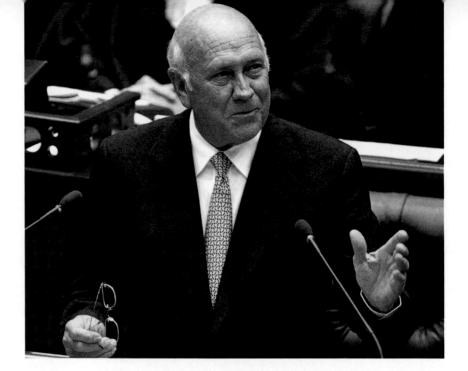

F. W. de Klerk addresses
Parliament.

> ## The End of Apartheid

In 1989, Botha was forced to resign. He was replaced by F. W.
de Klerk. Although de Klerk was an Afrikaner and loyal to
the National Party, he saw that the majority of the population
could not be denied their rights forever.

De Klerk understood that apartheid would have to end if
the country was going to survive. The only way to end apartheid was to talk with the leaders of the ANC, which meant
allowing the ANC to exist as an organization. As soon as he
took office, de Klerk began the process of ending apartheid.
In October 1989, he released important political prisoners to
test the reaction of the people. In February 1990, de Klerk
announced that the ANC, the PAC, and other organizations
representing blacks were no longer illegal. A few days later, on
February 11, 1990, Nelson Mandela was released from prison.
The ANC leader had been in jail for twenty-seven years.

South Africa was ready to enter the modern era. On March 17, 1992, de Klerk held a vote on a single question. He asked the whites, "Do you want us to continue the process of ending white rule in South Africa?" The answer was yes! By a margin of more than two to one, voters agreed that this was the right course.

De Klerk will always be remembered as the man who released Nelson Mandela from prison and paved the way for South Africa to have its first black president. Conservative Afrikaners see de Klerk as a traitor. But to most South Africans, including many Afrikaners, he had made an honorable decision. De Klerk and Mandela were jointly awarded the Nobel Peace Prize in 1993 for their work in ending apartheid peacefully.

### The Apartheid Museum

The Apartheid Museum in Johannesburg offers a powerful reminder of South Africa's bitter history. Visitors to the museum, which opened in 2001, buy tickets that indicate they are either "white" or "nonwhite." The museum preserves many artifacts of apartheid, including passbooks and prison cages.

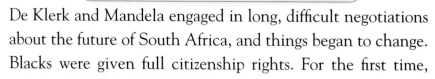

South Africans wait in line to cast their votes in the country's first democratic elections.

De Klerk and Mandela engaged in long, difficult negotiations about the future of South Africa, and things began to change. Blacks were given full citizenship rights. For the first time, everyone over the age of eighteen, no matter what their race, could vote.

South Africa's first democratic elections were held in April 1994. Millions of people voted for the first time in their lives. People waited in the hot sun for hours, some even all day, to cast that first ballot. Lines stretched for miles in some places. The voting was scheduled to take three days. At the last minute, an extra day was added to be sure everyone who wanted to could vote.

The ANC won the elections easily, and Nelson Mandela was chosen to be South Africa's first black president. He took over a country facing desperate problems, but filled with hope for the future.

## Nelson Mandela

South Africa's transition to democracy was only possible because of Nelson Mandela, whose belief that black people should have the same rights as white people cost him his freedom.

Mandela was born in 1918 in a small village in southeastern South Africa. His father was a leader of the Tembu people. Mandela attended the University of Fort Hare and later studied law. He and another man opened the first black law partnership in South Africa. Mandela joined the ANC in 1944 in hopes of overturning the nation's unjust laws. Soon the police were after him. The white South African government considered him a traitor because he spoke out against apartheid.

At his trial, he explained the ANC's decision to use violence if necessary to change South Africa. He said, "South Africa belongs to all the people who live in it, and not to one group, be it black or white. . . . I have cherished the ideal of a democratic and free society in which all persons live together in harmony and with equal opportunity. It is an ideal which I hope to live for and to achieve. But, if needs be, it is an ideal for which I am prepared to die."

Mandela became South Africa's most famous prisoner when he moved toward a more active opposition toward apartheid. Even from within the prison walls, he was able to influence others. He held talks with young black leaders, helping them shape their ideas. His strength of character helped him survive the long imprisonment.

When he was released from prison in 1990, he quickly reentered public life. Just four years later, Nelson Mandela was elected president of South Africa.

It is one of the most remarkable turnarounds in world politics. Though Mandela is no longer president, his moral vision, ideas, and actions still guide the nation as it tackles its many problems.

# A New
# Government

The END OF APARTHEID IN SOUTH AFRICA MEANT MORE than an end to legalized racial injustice. A new form of government had to be created. The nation's citizens could decide exactly the kind of a country they wanted South Africa to be. It was a unique opportunity, and they took full advantage of it.

*Opposite:* **Soldiers parade outside Parliament.**

## Writing a Constitution

On May 10, 1994, the new government went to work. Most of the members of government were black men and women.

**The South African National Assembly in session**

Many of them had to learn how to do their new jobs. There were tutors to teach members of Parliament how to enact laws and run the country.

The major task for lawmakers was writing a new constitution, or basic set of laws establishing how the country would be run. The lawmakers looked at constitutions used by countries all over the world. They took the parts they liked the best from each and then added many new ideas of their own.

One of the most important parts of the South African Constitution is the Bill of Rights, an idea taken from the U.S. Constitution. The rights guaranteed by the South African Constitution go far beyond those in the United States. They include the right to a healthy environment, housing, health care, food and water, and education. It protects against discrimination because of sexual orientation.

The guarantee of rights in the constitution does not mean that they will be granted quickly. It does mean that the government is committed to the goal of providing these rights to all citizens. This was the first time South Africa ever considered all its people to be citizens equally deserving of these rights.

President Mandela signed the new constitution into law on December 10, 1996, at Sharpeville. He chose that place as a way of honoring a pledge to guarantee personal freedom for all South Africans.

**South African president Nelson Mandela signs South Africa's new constitution.**

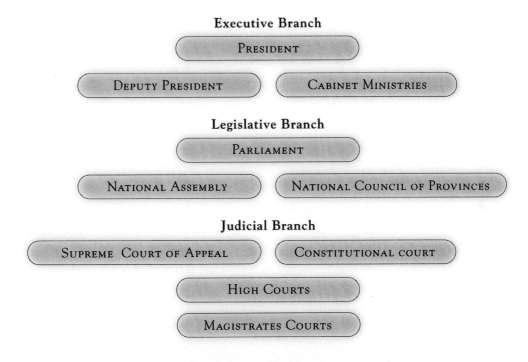

**NATIONAL GOVERNMENT OF SOUTH AFRICA**

Executive Branch
PRESIDENT
DEPUTY PRESIDENT    CABINET MINISTRIES

Legislative Branch
PARLIAMENT
NATIONAL ASSEMBLY    NATIONAL COUNCIL OF PROVINCES

Judicial Branch
SUPREME COURT OF APPEAL    CONSTITUTIONAL COURT
HIGH COURTS
MAGISTRATES COURTS

## *Parliamentary Government*

South Africa is governed according to a parliamentary system. Parliament is based in Cape Town and has two houses, the National Assembly and the National Council of Provinces. This is similar to the U.S. Senate and House of Representatives. The head of state is the president, who is chosen by members of Parliament and serves a five-year term.

## *The Judicial System*

South Africa's highest court for constitutional issues is the Constitutional Court. It deals with such matters as whether

**South Africans sit outside the Constitutional Court building.**

new laws follow the constitution. The Supreme Court of Appeal is the highest regular court in South Africa. It hears appeals from lower courts. Judges on both of these courts are appointed by the president.

## Provincial and Traditional Governments

South Africa has nine provinces, which are something like American states. Each province has a premier, who oversees a legislature that passes laws for that province. These laws must not conflict with national laws. The elected members of the provincial legislatures choose the premiers.

In addition to national, provincial, and local leaders, South Africa also recognizes traditional leaders. These are men and women who are chiefs of their communities. In the past, they were the only figures of authority. They upheld the laws of their people and had absolute power over their lives. They decided punishment for crimes, they allocated land, and they made treaties with other chiefdoms. Their authority was based on "customary" law, the law of the ethnic group. The country's new constitution recognizes their roles and allows them to act on matters that affect their own community.

### South Africa's Flag

The new South African flag combines red, black, white, green, blue, and yellow in a geometric design. The Y of the design represents separate groups merging into one unified nation. The colors come from other flags used in South Africa. The black, green, and yellow were popular with most of the black groups fighting for liberation from apartheid. The red, white, and blue appeared on flags from the colonial and settler periods.

This flag replaced one that had been used since 1928. That flag showed the British flag and the flags of two of the former Boer republics within three bands of color—orange, white, and blue. It reflected the origins of many of the nation's whites but did not represent blacks at all.

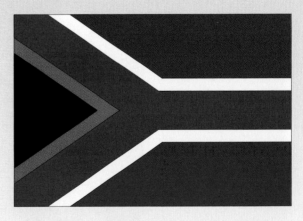

## The National Anthem

In 1897, a Xhosa teacher named Enoch Sontonga wrote a song called "Nkosi Sikelel' iAfrika," (Lord Bless Africa). It became the anthem of the African National Congress.

In 1994, when all South Africans were free to choose their president in the first national elections, "Nkosi Sikelel' iAfrika" became the country's national anthem. It shares the stage with the former anthem of South Africans under Afrikaner rule, "Die Stem van Suid-Afrika" (The Call of South Africa).

**Zulu lyrics**

Nkosi, sikelel' iAfrika,
Malupnakanyisw' udumo lwayo;
Yizwa imithandazo yethu
Nkosi sikelela,
Nkosi sikelela,

Nkosi, sikelel' iAfrika,
Malupnakanyisw' udumo lwayo;
Yizwa imithandazo yethu
Nkosi sikelela,
Nkosi sikelela,

Woza Moya (woza, woza),
Woza Moya (woza, woza),
Woza Moya, Oyingcwele.
Usisikelele,
Thina lusapho lwayo.

**English lyrics**

Lord, bless Africa
May her spirit rise high up
Hear thou our prayers
Lord, bless us.

Lord, bless Africa
May her spirit rise high up
Hear thou our prayers
Lord, bless us
Your family.

Chorus
Descend, O Spirit
Descend, O Holy Spirit
Lord, bless us
Your family.
(Repeat)

South African children sing their national anthem.

## The Truth and Reconciliation Commission

In 1995, the government appointed the Truth and Reconciliation Commission to look into terrible crimes committed during apartheid. Archbishop Desmond Tutu, a civil rights leader and Anglican priest, was chosen to head the commission. South Africa's former white rulers, the police, and the army had committed many acts of terrorism. They had tortured and murdered people. They had been responsible for depriving people of the most basic human rights. Some atrocities had also been committed by people trying to end apartheid.

The South African government created the commission to find a way to bring former enemies together. People who wanted to confess to crimes they had committed could appear before the committee and face members of the family involved. The families would finally know what had really happened.

In 1997, the commission began two years of hearings. Tutu and the other commission members traveled all over the country. They heard horrible tales of violence and an outpouring of sorrow and grief. Day after day, people at the hearings wept as they listened to the stories of the victims and those who tortured them.

Tutu believed that the stories needed to be told before anyone could begin to forgive the people who committed the crimes. He believed that forgiveness was necessary for South Africa to advance as a nation. The commission helped the nation heal the past and move forward.

## South Africa's Capitals

South Africa is unusual in that it has three capital cities: a legislative capital, an administrative capital, and a judicial capital.

Cape Town (page 63, top right), the legislative capital of South Africa, is home to Parliament. Parliament makes the laws. Cape Town is a beautiful city with a long history. It was the home of the region's first Dutch settlers. Their influence can still be seen in some of the architecture. Located on the Atlantic coast, Cape Town is a major seaport. Though it has a pleasant climate most of the year and its beaches are beautiful, few people venture into the cold ocean waters.

Pretoria, which is also called Tshwane, is the administrative capital of South Africa.

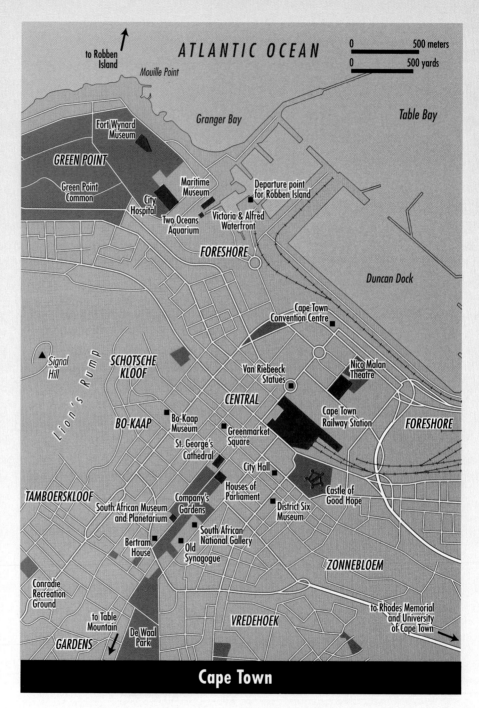

to Robben Island

Mouille Point

ATLANTIC OCEAN

Granger Bay

Table Bay

0  500 meters
0  500 yards

Fort Wynard Museum

GREEN POINT

Green Point Common

Maritime Museum

City Hospital

Two Oceans Aquarium

Departure point for Robben Island

Victoria & Alfred Waterfront

FORESHORE

Duncan Dock

Cape Town Convention Centre

Signal Hill

SCHOTSCHE KLOOF

Van Riebeeck Statues

Nico Malan Theatre

CENTRAL

Cape Town Railway Station

FORESHORE

BO-KAAP

Bo-Kaap Museum

Greenmarket Square

St. George's Cathedral

City Hall

Houses of Parliament

Castle of Good Hope

TAMBOERSKLOOF

Company's Gardens

South African Museum and Planetarium

District Six Museum

Bertram House

South African National Gallery

Old Synagogue

ZONNEBLOEM

Conradie Recreation Ground

to Table Mountain

De Waal Park

VREDEHOEK

to Rhodes Memorial and University of Cape Town

GARDENS

**Cape Town**

Government sessions are held in the Union Building (right) that lies on a hilltop overlooking the city. The president and the cabinet members meet here. Pretoria was once considered an Afrikaans city, and it was rare to hear any other language there. Today, however, Pretoria's cosmopolitan population reflects the changes in South Africa. Spring is the loveliest time of year in Pretoria. The jacaranda trees that line the main streets blossom with bright, fragrant purple flowers.

Bloemfontein is the judicial capital. It is the site of the Supreme Court of Appeal, the highest court in the country. Bloemfontein is a pleasant town, perhaps most famous as the birthplace of J. R. R. Tolkein, the author of the Lord of the Rings series.

CHAPTER

SIX

# The Powerhouse of Africa

S OUTH AFRICA IS THE ECONOMIC POWERHOUSE OF THE African continent. Though it occupies just 4 percent of the land and has only 6 percent of the population, it creates 25 percent of the continent's wealth and has 40 percent of the industry on the entire continent.

*Opposite:* **A furnace blazes at a South African platinum factory.**

**A woman sorts diamonds in Kimberley.**

### An Economy Built on Minerals

Sometimes people say that a wealthy city has "streets paved with gold." In Johannesburg, this is nearly true. The city was built on the site of South Africa's greatest gold vein. South Africa is also rich in diamonds and is the world's biggest supplier of platinum. Platinum is used to make jewelry. It is also a vital part of pollution-control devices used in automobiles.

South African gold mines in total employ about two hundred thousand, down from a high of more than five hundred thousand in 1987. And its huge mineral reserves ensure that it will continue to provide people with jobs for decades to come. South Africa has about 46 percent of all the gold reserves in the world, more than half the platinum reserves, and nearly three-quarters of all the chromium reserves. De Beers, the best-known South African company, mines diamonds throughout the region, though the reserves are much smaller. De Beers controls the marketing of about 50 percent of all the diamonds mined in the world.

South Africa also has many factories. Chemicals, metal products, cars, and processed foods are among its top manufactured items.

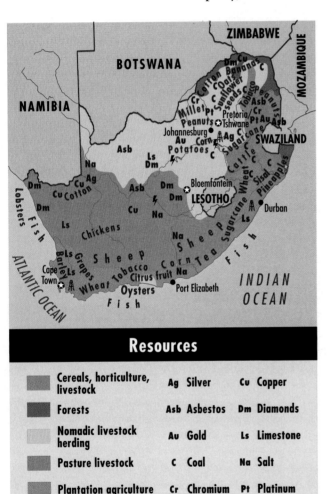

## Resources

| | | |
|---|---|---|
| Cereals, horticulture, livestock | Ag Silver | Cu Copper |
| Forests | Asb Asbestos | Dm Diamonds |
| Nomadic livestock herding | Au Gold | Ls Limestone |
| Pasture livestock | C Coal | Na Salt |
| Plantation agriculture | Cr Chromium | Pt Platinum |
| ⚡ Hydroelectric power | ⛏ Oil | |

### Agriculture

Though farming once occupied most South Africans, today it accounts for only 4 percent of the country's economy. Most people in the rural areas grow food for their own use. This can be difficult because South Africa gets little rain. Large-scale farmers, most of them white, grow huge amounts of food for sale at market. They have an easier time because they have better land and better equipment.

The single most important crop in South Africa is corn, which is used to make flour. South Africa also produces beef and dairy cattle, chickens and eggs, apples, and wheat. Grapes are another important crop. Some of these grapes are used to make wine.

## Working in the Mines

Mines need huge numbers of workers to bring out the ore. Working underground is very tough. Miners work in hot, humid, and dangerous tunnels. They don't see the sky or breathe fresh air all day long.

Most black miners come to the mines to earn money and then go back to their homes, often hundreds of miles away. These migrant workers often don't see their families for six months or more at a time. With the rise of mining, migratory labor became the pattern of life for hundreds of thousands of Africans. Today, some miners bring their families with them to the mining regions.

Being a miner is a hazardous job. Mining accidents claim lives every year. On average, one miner is killed for every ton of gold produced. Sometimes there are

cave-ins at the mining site. Other times, a mine elevator fails. These huge elevators take the miners deep down into the earth and can hold up to one hundred men. Most of the elevators and mine shafts are very old.

## Cyril Ramaphosa

Cyril Ramaphosa, a black lawyer, came to the public eye in 1984 as leader of the National Union of Mineworkers (NUM). Ramaphosa worked to earn pay raises and better working conditions for the miners. Because of his skill as a negotiator, he was named to lead the committee to write the country's new constitution. When the constitution was completed, he moved into the business world. He now directs Johnnies Industrial Corp., which is nicknamed Johnnic.

South Africa is the ninth-largest wine producer in the world. Most of the nation's vineyards are located near Cape Town. Traditionally, most of the winery workers were Coloureds. Now blacks also work in the vineyards, although the managers are nearly all white.

**Robertson Vineyards, Western Cape Province**

Visitors watch a white rhinocerus at the Lapalala Wilderness Reserve.

## Tourism

One of the brightest areas of employment since the end of apartheid is the tourist industry. Since 1994, the number of people coming to South Africa has grown from 640,000 to 6.5 million per year. This number includes both tourists and businesspeople who travel to and from the country regularly. Wildlife parks are the biggest attraction. But visitors also come for the resorts, casinos, beaches, and other sites.

Cape Town brings many visitors to the country, both for tourism and business. It offers dramatic scenery as well as first-class hotels and restaurants. The Cape Town Convention Centre, which opened in 2003, brings thousands of business visitors to the city. The Convention Centre is located at the entrance to the Victoria & Alfred Waterfront, the most visited spot in South Africa. A waterway connects the two sites, making it easy for tourists and businesspeople to travel back and forth. Forty major hotels have been built in Cape Town

**Visitors at the Shamwari Private Game Reserve, a traditional African village for tourists**

since 1994. The skyline is always full of construction cranes.

Cultural tourism is one of the newest trends in South Africa. Re-created "villages" offer a chance to experience traditional African life. Shakaland, in KwaZulu-Natal, was created from the location for the television series *Shaka Zulu*. Here visitors can watch Zulu dances, eat authentic foods, and learn about Zulu fighting techniques and weapons. At Lesedi, less than an hour's drive from Johannesburg, the dance and costumes of various South African groups are demonstrated. Because few tourists are able to visit traditional people in rural areas, these cultural villages are the next best way to learn how some South Africans live.

Investment in tourist facilities is key to South Africa's economic future. The St. Lucia wetlands are one of the most important natural resources in the country. A plan to develop a mine in the region was stopped by environmental activists. Now the government is hoping the Greater St. Lucia Wetland Park will become one of the biggest tourist attractions in the country. Investments in tourist facilities to serve the park would create about two thousand long-term jobs.

While there are millions of black South Africans who need jobs, few of them have been educated for the business world. It will take many years for blacks to make up for the education and experience they were once denied.

The number of black South Africans in professional positions is small, but it is growing rapidly. Telkom is one firm that has worked hard to create jobs for blacks. Telkom is South Africa's telephone company. In 1993, at the tail end of the apartheid era, the company had one black employee out of 58,000 people. Within two years, it had hired nearly one hundred black managers. While the government doesn't set quotas on hiring blacks, it awards contracts only to companies that can show they have made progress in adding blacks to their workforce.

## What South Africa Grows, Makes, and Mines

**Agriculture**

| | |
|---|---|
| Poultry | 163,791,185 chickens sold |
| Beef cattle | 2,728,032 head of cattle sold |
| Corn | 9,700,000 tons produced |

**Manufacturing** *(in U.S. dollars)*

| | |
|---|---|
| Chemicals | 1,633,400,000 |
| Processed foods and beverages | 1,627,600,000 |
| Iron and steel | 1,331,600,000 |

**Mining**

| | |
|---|---|
| Gold | 451 tons mined (1999) |
| Diamonds | 12.8 million carats (2003) |
| Coal | 223.4 million tons (2001) |

Under apartheid, blacks were not allowed to attend the same kind of classes as whites. Because of this at least 7.5 million South African adults are illiterate. Only 14 percent of the black adult population and 17 percent of the Coloured adult population have completed high school. This means that many people are still working as maids and gardeners. They don't enjoy benefits such as health care, and they don't have a chance to save money and to build better lives.

### South African Currency

The South African unit of currency is called the rand. It is named after the ridge of land where South Africa's gold mines are found. In 2005, a rand was worth about fifteen cents in American money. One rand is divided into one hundred cents.

Coins range in value from one cent to five rand. The five-rand coin shows a bucking wildebeest (right). Each banknote is a different size depending on its value. The smallest bill is worth ten rand; the largest is two hundred rand. Each is also a different color, so it is easy to tell the bills apart. All of the bills feature the country's wildlife. The fifty-rand note, which is pink, shows a lion.

South Africa needs tremendous amounts of money to build factories and create new jobs. After the end of apartheid, businesspeople and newly elected officials lost no time in traveling to foreign countries, trying to interest companies in investing in South Africa.

The investments began in 1991, when sanctions against South Africa ended. Within a few years, U.S. companies alone had invested more than $1 billion in South Africa. Half of that money came from manufacturing companies such as the Ford Motor Company and Levi Strauss blue jeans. More than 350 U.S. companies have now invested in South Africa. The Levi's factory in Epping, an industrial area near Cape Town, employs 230 workers, most of them women.

Many American companies operate in South Africa.

One of the surest signs of South Africa's economic recovery was the appearance of McDonald's fast food restaurants. When the first McDonald's opened in South Africa in 1995, it made front-page news in the local newspapers. On opening day, twenty thousand people were served at one of the new restaurants in Johannesburg. There are now McDonald's restaurants in many cities.

The Powerhouse of Africa **73**

Despite foreign investments, many people still cannot find steady jobs. An estimated two million people earn some kind of living in the "informal sector." This includes people who make crafts or bake breads, as well as people who sit on the sidewalks selling a tiny stock of gum or candies. Some have small shops, called spaza shops, in the black communities. They sell a variety of items, including groceries. Under apartheid, spaza shops were often the only places where residents of townships could shop without traveling to white-owned stores in the cities. The combined sale of all these small shops and street vendors amounts to about 7 percent of the nation's economic output.

Vendors display their goods at the Grahamstown Craft Market.

Sidewalk vendors sit outside, in hot weather and in the rain, waiting for customers. These hawkers, as they are called, reflect one of the most visible changes in South African cities. There was a time, in the most conservative towns, when black people were expected to step off the sidewalk and into the street to allow a white person to pass by. Now the sidewalks in some cities more closely resemble those in other parts of Africa.

A lively crafts market can be found outside in Greenmarket Square, in the heart of Cape Town. It's an ideal place for vendors because it gets a steady stream of tourists every day. In Durban, female street vendors have formed their own union, the Self-Employed Women's Union, to protect their rights. The cities now truly reflect the population of South Africa.

## Modernizing Utilities

In South Africa, phone service is available and dependable in the white areas and in the wealthier black areas. But in many poor and rural areas, there is no phone service at all. The country is trying to bring phone service to these areas. In some cases, only cell phone systems are being installed, because they are less expensive than land lines.

## The Port of Durban

South Africa's major port city, Durban, on the Indian Ocean, serves much of southern Africa. Its modern facilities are well maintained. It is a reliable port, where shippers know their goods will not sit out on the docks until they spoil in the sun. This often happens in ports in other countries along the same coast. Rail lines carry goods from the port all over southern Africa.

The Maputo Corridor, a land route that links the port of Maputo in Mozambique to Johannesburg, provides an alternative to the port at Durban. It is an example of the cooperation that is possible since South Africa became democratic.

**Weights and Measures**

South Africa uses the metric system. In the metric system, length is measured in meters. One meter is equal to about 3.2 feet. Weight is measured in kilograms. One kilogram equals about 2.2 pounds.

# A Land of Many Languages

**CHAPTER SEVEN**

76

L ANGUAGE IS A UNIFYING FORCE FOR MOST NATIONS. BUT in South Africa, language was long used as a tool to control and separate people. Today, South Africa celebrates the many languages spoken there. For the first time, black African languages are recognized as having a place in business, government, and daily life.

According to the nation's constitution, the official languages of South Africa are: Sepedi, Sesotho, Setswana, siSwati, Tshivenda, Xitsonga, Afrikaans, English, isiNdebele, isiXhosa,

*Opposite:* **A Xhosa woman in traditional clothing**

**Many South African teenagers speak more than one language.**

and isiZulu. English, the language of business, is the only official language that is used internationally. Afrikaans is spoken throughout the country by Afrikaners, Coloureds, and many people who learned it in school. The constitution also recognizes the languages spoken by the Khoikhoi, Nama, and San peoples, as well as sign language.

Both the national government and the provincial government must use at least two of the official languages in official business. Citizens in any area of the country can expect to speak their own language when dealing with the government.

The nine official "black" languages in South Africa all belong to the same major branch of Bantu languages. But each is spoken by a distinct group of Africans. For example, isiZulu is spoken by the Zulu people who dominate the province of KwaZulu-Natal, but it is also spoken by Zulus wherever they live.

## Ethnic South Africa

The black African population in South Africa numbers about 30 million people. The largest group is the Zulus, who number about 9 million, followed by the Xhosa, who number about 7 million. There are an estimated 3.5 million Pedi, 3.4 million Tswana, 2.7 million Southern Sotho, 1.8 million Tsonga, 1 million Swazi, 900,000 Venda, and 600,000 Ndebele. The white population breaks down into Afrikaners, who number about 3 million, and English speakers, who number about 2 million. South Africa is also home to about 4 million Coloured people, many of whom speak Afrikaans as their first language. Finally, South Africa has about 1 million people of Asian descent, such as Indians, Malay, and Chinese, who speak English or Afrikaans as well as an Asian language.

| Ethnic Breakdown of South Africa | |
| --- | --- |
| Black | 79.0% |
| White | 9.6% |
| Coloured | 8.9% |
| Indian/Asian | 2.5% |

### Changing Languages

Languages do not stay the same. Change may come when words are needed for new technologies. Sometimes words from another language are adopted because they describe an activity so well. The Afrikaans word *trek*, for example, has become part of everyday English.

A young Xhosa woman in South Africa

The Xhosas are the second-largest ethnic group in South Africa after the Zulus. IsiXhosa is the first language of Nelson Mandela. It is known to Westerners as a "click" language because it includes "pops," or clicks, when it is spoken. The "X" stands for a click sound.

Many Xhosas and Zulus have moved to the cities looking for work. A large Xhosa population lives in the Cape Flats area near Cape Town. Many Zulus live in

**A Zulu man in traditional dress**

Soweto, South Africa's biggest black township. But Xhosas, Tswanas, and people of other language groups also live there. As they mix, these people tend to learn each other's language. Most people in Soweto speak several languages. In Soweto, the casual mixing of languages, especially among young people, has led to a special township dialect. In the province of Gauteng, which includes Soweto, five languages are sometimes used in a single household.

Many Pedi, Tswana, and Sotho people live in the northeastern part of the country. People who speak their languages also make up the population of neighboring countries. Tswana-speaking people live in Botswana. Sotho-speaking people live in the country of Lesotho. SiSwati is spoken by the Swazi people who live in the South African province of Mpumalanga. It is the same language spoken by the people of Swaziland. Each of these ethnic groups was split up when the countries' boundaries were drawn by Europeans.

Many educated adults in the Coloured community speak both English and Afrikaans and can easily switch back and forth. Because English is the language of business, many Afrikaners are also fluent in English. English speakers, however, are much less likely to be fluent in Afrikaans. In meetings, speakers often alternate between two languages. In films and plays, it's common to have the actors speak more than one language. South Africa is truly a multilingual nation.

The languages used on television have changed dramatically since 1990. Once there were two channels, one in English and one in Afrikaans. Now the news may be in Zulu or Xhosa, English or Afrikaans. On some news programs, interviewers may speak one language while the person being interviewed answers in another language. In some places, the constant mixing of English and Afrikaans has resulted in a dialect called *kombuis Afrikaans*, which means "kitchen Afrikaans."

| Population of South Africa's Largest Cities (2001) | |
| --- | --- |
| Johannesburg | 3,225,812 |
| Cape Town | 2,893,215 |
| Durban | 2,117,650 |
| Pretoria/Tshwane | 1,104,479 |
| Port Elizabeth | 749,921 |

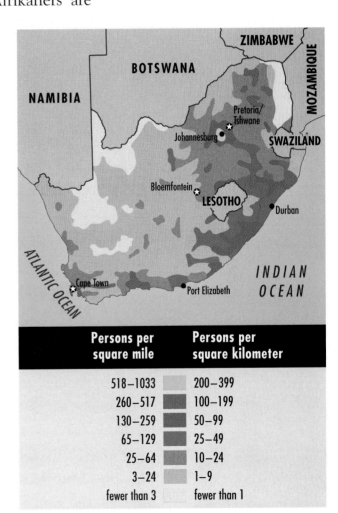

| Persons per square mile | Persons per square kilometer |
| --- | --- |
| 518–1033 | 200–399 |
| 260–517 | 100–199 |
| 130–259 | 50–99 |
| 65–129 | 25–49 |
| 25–64 | 10–24 |
| 3–24 | 1–9 |
| fewer than 3 | fewer than 1 |

**Malays march to a mosque in Cape Town.**

## Ethnic Relations

Since the end of apartheid, the races have been allowed to mix, legally. In some areas, especially cities, people of different races use the same restaurants, attend the same schools, and work together in business. Blacks who are earning higher incomes often buy homes in formerly white neighborhoods. But the vast majority of South Africans still live in racially separate regions, much as they did before.

People remain separated by their cultures. Although Afrikaners and English-speaking whites are the same color, they often enjoy different foods and entertainment. South Africans of Asian descent remain separate from both the whites and the blacks. Indians maintain a strong cultural identity and rarely marry non-Indians. The much smaller Malay population also maintains a strong, separate cultural identity. The Malays prefer to live in the same neighborhood as their family members.

## New Immigrants

Since apartheid ended, South Africa has become a beacon of hope for desperate people living in neighboring countries. Millions of refugees have flowed into South Africa from the poor country of Mozambique and from the country of Zimbabwe, which suffers under a ruler whose policies have destroyed the economy. These new immigrants compete with South Africans for jobs. These immigrants are not registered with the government and are not counted in the population. It is estimated that the true population of South Africa is at least five million more than the official number.

**About 40 percent of the South African workforce is without a job.**

# Spiritual Lives

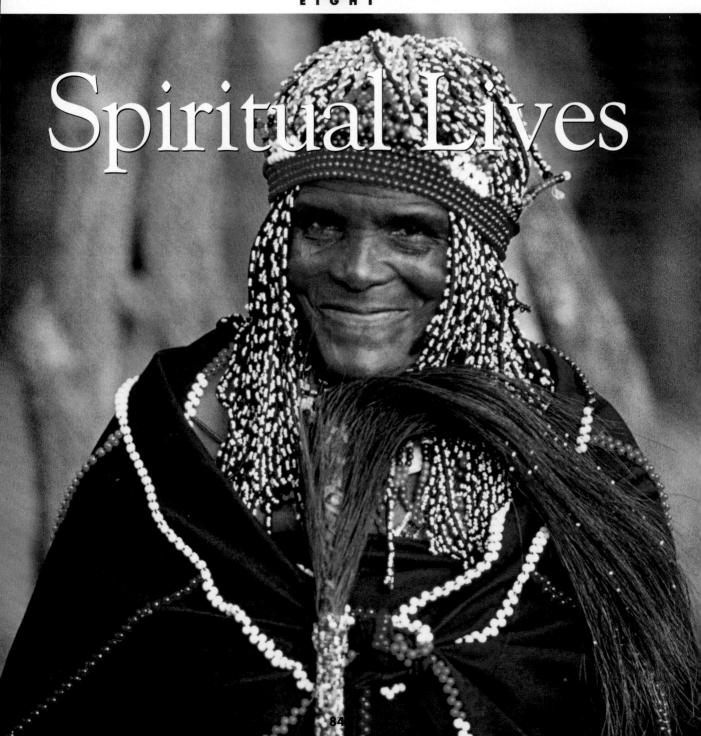

RELIGION PLAYS AN IMPORTANT ROLE IN SOUTH AFRICAN life. About three-quarters of all South Africans are Christians, most of them Protestants. About eight million South Africans attend African Independent churches. Services in these churches combine Protestant beliefs with traditional African practices. Another four million attend other Protestant churches including Methodist, Anglican, Lutheran, and

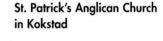

*Opposite:* **A Zulu traditional healer**

**St. Patrick's Anglican Church in Kokstad**

South African Catholics mourn Pope John Paul II's death.

Presbyterian. Among whites and Coloured people, the largest Protestant denomination is the Dutch Reformed Church, with about four million members. Virtually all of the world's religions are practiced in South Africa. There are Roman Catholics, Mormons, Hindus, Muslims, and a small number of Jews.

### Traditional Beliefs

Many people in South Africa do not follow a formal, church-based religion, but they do have strong religious beliefs. A person's ancestors—father, mother, aunts, uncles, and all the people who came before them—are considered part of the living community. They are believed to play a role in the direction of daily life. They are thought to influence whether a person has good luck or bad luck. Some people combine their traditional beliefs with Christian practices.

## Traditional Healers

Part of traditional beliefs in South Africa is relying on traditional healers called sangomas. Sangomas are called to their profession, often in a dream. Many are women, and they are easily identified by their distinctive headdress. Beads often fall in front of a sangoma's face, so others are not able to get a clear view of her. The sangoma tells of events that will affect a person's life in the future.

Spiritual and physical well-being are closely connected in African life. People ask their traditional healers for medicines to cure their problems as well as their illnesses. Traditional healers know their patients well, because they live in the same community. They take the patient's entire history into consideration and can be quite skilled in pinpointing a person's disease or illness.

A sangoma healer in traditional dress

About two hundred thousand traditional healers practice in South Africa. Many have a wide knowledge of natural medicines such as herbs and tree roots. The plants they prescribe are now being studied by drug companies. About 84 percent of South Africans consult sangomas. For most South Africans, they are the only medical help available. The government is planning to license sangomas just as they do druggists.

## The Dutch Reformed Church

The separation of church and state—the belief that government should not be involved with religion—is a new idea in South Africa. Under the white government, the Dutch Reformed Church was the church of the National Party.

A Dutch Reformed Church in Swellendam, at the foot of the Langeberg Mountains

The Dutch Reformed Church arrived in South Africa in 1652 with the first Dutch settlers. It is a strict form of Christianity, with no singing or joyfulness, and its services are held in buildings without decoration. The Afrikaner members of the Dutch Reformed Church held a narrow interpretation of the Bible. They used their interpretation to justify apartheid.

In addition to whites, about 750,000 Coloureds belong to the Dutch Reformed Church. Most speak Afrikaans as their first language, giving them strong ties to the Afrikaner community. But the Coloured members of the church broke with the Afrikaners on the subject of apartheid, declaring it a sin.

The end of apartheid stunned many devout Afrikaners. They had lived their lives according to the teachings of their church. Apartheid had been a core element of their lives, and they had to admit that the church's teachings were wrong. Many left the church in despair. Others insisted that apartheid was right and broke away from the main Dutch Reformed Church, joining even more conservative churches.

## The Zion Christian Church

The Zion Christian Church is the fastest-growing religious movement in South Africa. Founded in 1910 by Engenas Lekganyane, the church counts a membership of more than five million black South Africans. The Zion Christian Church has a strong Christian core, adjusted to suit the way these Africans choose to worship. For example, they permit polygamy, the practice of having more than one wife at a time.

**Religious Beliefs in South Africa**

| | |
|---|---|
| Christian | 68% |
| Indigenous religions | 28% |
| Muslim | 2% |
| Hindu | 1.5% |
| Jewish | 0.2% |

**Members of the Zion Christian Church perform a baptism in the Indian Ocean near Durban.**

They do not permit smoking, drinking alcohol, or eating pork. They feel very close connections to their ancestors, as do most traditional African peoples.

Although some Zionists accept Western medicine, they put most of their trust in faith healing, the belief that faith is the strongest medicine of all. They are vigorously opposed to sangomas, the traditional African healers.

## Archbishop Desmond Tutu

In South Africa during apartheid, one church leader stood out for his willingness to speak up. Anglican Archbishop Desmond Mpilo Tutu turned his pulpit into a platform opposing apartheid.

Tutu was born in Klerksdorp in 1931. The son of a teacher, he became a teacher as well. He was working at a high school in Johannesburg when the Bantu Education Act was passed. Tutu quit in protest and turned his attention to religion. He became an Anglican priest in 1960.

As a moral and spiritual leader, Tutu questioned the morals of the leaders of the National Party, who were Christians. When the government wrote a new constitution in 1983, which gave limited rights to Coloureds and Asians but not to blacks, Tutu spoke out against it. He also spoke in favor of economic sanctions against South Africa. Tutu's work opposing apartheid earned him the Nobel Peace Prize in 1984. Two years later, the Anglican Church named him archbishop of South Africa, despite the fact that black and white church members could not attend the same services.

After apartheid ended, Tutu headed the Truth and Reconciliation Commission looking into human rights abuses. Although he has retired as archbishop, he remains a strong voice in support of freedom and human rights around the world.

Other religions are also important in South Africa. The Malay community, who are descended from slaves brought to South Africa more than three hundred years ago, are devout Muslims. Although the Dutch did not allow them to practice their religion, they managed to keep their beliefs alive through the centuries. The first Muslim mosque was built in 1798, in Cape Town. Members of the Malay community do not drink alcohol or eat pork.

**Chiappini Street in Bo-Kaap**

During apartheid, most Malay were forced to leave their homes on the slopes of Table Mountain in Cape Town and go to the Cape Flats. A small group managed to stay on in a section called Bo-Kaap. Bo-Kaap is known for its brightly painted homes nestled on steep streets. The area is so desirable that today many outsiders have bought homes there and are changing the character of the neighborhood. The Muslim residents are often forced to move as city property taxes increase beyond their means.

The Indians who were brought to South Africa in the
1860s as laborers on sugarcane plantations also brought their
own religions with them. Most are Hindus, but some are
Muslim. Today, Durban is the center of the Asian community
in South Africa. Many Hindu temples and Muslim mosques
were built there to meet the needs of the growing community.
People from the two religions rarely marry, though they share
a common ethnic heritage.

The first Jewish synagogue in South Africa was built in
Cape Town in 1863. Most South African Jews are descended
from Lithuanians who fled religious persecution in Europe
in the late 1800s. The earliest arrivals lived in District Six,
where the last Jewish bookstore still stands amid the rubble.
The community grew to about one hundred twenty thousand
by the 1970s. Today, about eighty thousand Jews make South
Africa their home. Most live in the suburbs of Johannesburg
and Cape Town.

# Rich
# Traditions

F ROM THE FOOT-STOMPING GUMBOOT DANCE OF THE ZULUS to classical symphonies and ballet, South Africans enjoy a wide variety of music, dance, art, and theater. Because of the enormous number of languages used in the country, many cultural activities are enjoyed only by those who speak a certain language.

*Opposite:* **South Africans march in a carnival parade.**

**The Broomhill Opera Company at the Spier Festival**

One thing that unites the entire country is a love of sports. South Africa is a nation that is sports crazy. During apartheid, the country was banned from most international sports competitions. It had not participated in the Olympics since 1960. This denied young people the chance to compete against the best in the world. Some South African athletes gave up their citizenship and moved to other countries to be able to compete. Sydney Maree, a brilliant runner, became a U.S. citizen and competed for the United States in the 1980s. He returned to South Africa in the 1990s to head a sporting company. Many others could not afford to leave or were not willing to leave their homes and families.

**Boys play soccer in a field near Transkei.**

In 1991, as apartheid was coming to an end, the Olympic committee announced that South Africa would again be allowed to compete. It was barely a year before the 1992 Games, not enough time to put together a full, multiracial team. Still, 120 South African athletes and staff went to the Summer Olympics in Barcelona, Spain. Nearly all were white, since blacks had little access to sports training and facilities under apartheid. But the team brought home one medal. Runner Elana Meyer won the silver medal in the 10,000-meter race.

In 1995, South Africa hosted the World Rugby

South African athlete Elana Meyer in the 10,000-meter race at the 1992 Olympic Games

Cup competition. The South African team had just one black player among the whites. Against all odds, South Africa won the World Cup, beating heavily favored New Zealand. After

**South African rugby player
Jaco Pretorius tries to dodge
a Uruguayan player.**

the victory, people danced in the streets, blacks and whites celebrating together. The motto for the event was One Team, One Nation.

Despite this success, rugby remains primarily a white sport in South Africa. Blacks all over Africa are much more excited by soccer. South Africa's soccer team soon proved it was up to the task of uniting the nation. In 1996, when the team won the African Cup of Nations for the first time, the leading player was a Coloured named Mark Williams.

It was a moment of pure joy across South Africa in 2004 when it was announced that the nation would host soccer's World Cup in 2010. The World Cup is the single most popular sports event in the world. Hosting it is a great honor for South Africa. The news brought people of all races out to celebrate. Thirty-two of the world's best teams will compete in stadiums throughout South Africa. The event is expected to be the biggest tourist attraction the nation has ever seen. It will also create many new jobs as facilities are built for the games.

Joseph S. Blatter of FIFA, the international soccer organization, announces South Africa as the host of the 2010 World Cup.

In recent years, South Africa has become more and more successful in international sports competitions. In August 2004, South African athletes won six medals at the Olympic Games in Athens, Greece. In swimming, the South African team shocked the United States, taking gold in the 4 x 100-meter relay. Roland Schoeman, who was part of that team, also won a silver medal in the men's 100-meter freestyle swimming event and a bronze in the 50-meter freestyle. Mbulaeni Mulaudzi won a silver medal in the men's 800-meter track race, while Hestrie Cloete took silver in the women's high jump. The South African rowing team also took home one bronze medal.

The Cape Argus Cycle Tour is the biggest one-day sporting event in the country. During this event, more than 35,000 cyclists race a difficult course around Cape Town's mountains for a distance of 68 miles (109 km). The tour draws competitors from around the world, while more than 200,000 people line the course to watch.

The South Atlantic Race, a treacherous yacht race across the Atlantic Ocean, is held every three years. The yachts set off from Cape Town's harbor with Table Mountain in the background. Three or four weeks later, they reach the finish line in Rio de Janeiro, Brazil.

**Cyclists climb Suikerbossie Hill in the annual Cape Argus Cycle Tour near Cape Town.**

A performance by the South African hip-hop group Black Noise

## Music

From the most traditional music to the hip-hop of today, South African artists perform for a variety of tastes. One of the most popular hip-hop groups in South Africa is called Black Noise. Their songs express the reality of township life, gangs, drug abuse, and unemployment. They perform in a combination of English and Afrikaans as well as slang that is familiar in the Cape Flats. This sometimes confusing combination of languages is a perfect example of the complicated cultural scene. Their lyrics talk about racism, past and present. The group is also active in social issues, lending a helping hand to South Africa's youth.

**Joseph Shabalala, leader of the singing group Ladysmith Black Mambazo, celebrates the sugarcane harvest with a group of Zulu dancers.**

Choral singing, without musical accompaniment, highlights some of South Africa's best voices. Groups compete to win prizes and recognition. The best-known choral group from South Africa is Ladysmith Black Mambazo, led by Joseph Shabalala. Their sweet harmony is now recognized around the world.

For most South Africans who live in rural areas, radio provides all the entertainment and information. Radio programs are offered in a wide variety of languages, tailored to each local area. News, weather, entertainment, and many kinds of educational programs fill the airwaves. Most people listen on battery-operated radios.

### Zulu Culture

What does it mean to be a Zulu? That is a question musician Johnny Clegg has been asked throughout his career. Although Clegg is white, he is known for his Zulu songs and for dancing the thundering foot-stomping dance of the Zulus. Clegg was sixteen years old when he became friendly with some Zulu musicians. Throughout the years, he studied and then taught anthropology. At the same time, he absorbed the Zulu music, language, and culture. He has spent his life performing Zulu music and dance. He and guitarist Sipho Mchunu formed a musical group called Juluka (which means "sweat"). Their act was a defiant symbol during apartheid: A black gardener and a white university student were not supposed to share a culture.

## The Coloureds' Carnival

Each year on January 2, hundreds of Coloured people take to the streets of Cape Town to celebrate the annual Coloureds' Carnival. Groups of people paint their faces, wear matching costumes, and carry tiny, colorful umbrellas as they dance and sing their way through town.

The Coloureds' Carnival owes much of its look and sound to American traditions. In the 1800s, American ships stopped at Cape Town. The local people quickly picked up the sailors' music and imitated it. During the worst years of apartheid, the Coloureds were not allowed to parade through the streets. Instead, they had to hold their celebration in a stadium. Since the end of apartheid, their joyful parade has again reclaimed the streets.

## Literature

The complex racial relations in South Africa and the horrors of apartheid have given the nation's writers rich material to work with. The most famous South African novel is Alan Paton's *Cry, the Beloved Country*. The book, which was published in 1948, shined a bright light on the nation's violent racism.

Two South African writers have won the Nobel Prize for Literature. Nadine Gordimer won the prize in 1991, and J. M. Coetzee won it in 2003. Coetzee, an Afrikaner by heritage,

*Above left:* **South African author Nadine Gordimer**

*Above right:* **J. M. Coetzee receiving the Nobel Prize for Literature in 2003**

was awarded the prize for his novels, which explore the apartheid system and its impact on South Africa. Born in 1940, Coetzee was raised in an Afrikaans-speaking household, but he attended an English-speaking school and writes his books in English. Although Coetzee's books are all centered on the impact of apartheid, he has lived outside of South Africa for many years. Among his many books are In *the Heart of the Country, Waiting for the Barbarians, Disgrace,* and *The Life and Times of Michael K.*

One of the most prominent black South African writers is Zakes Mda. He first gained attention as a playwright in the 1970s. In recent years, he has turned his attention to novels. Works such as *The Ways of Dying* and *The Heart of Redness* bring in elements of magic.

## Art and Artists

The South African National Gallery in Cape Town offers exhibits of both African and European art. It is located right in the Company Gardens, where Jan van Riebeeck began growing food for the first people who came to Africa from Holland. On display are works by Willie Bester, South Africa's best-known artist. Bester, who was born in 1956, often uses recycled materials in his sculptures and paintings.

*Homage to Steve Biko* by Willie Bester

In District Six, a church has been turned into a museum that commemorates the community that was destroyed. Hanging from the ceiling are some of the old street signs: Hanover Street, Reform Street, Springfield Street, de Korte Street, Van de Leur Street. The man responsible for directing the destruction of the district could not bear to throw the signs away. He hid them in his basement for twenty years and then gave them to the museum. A map on the floor shows all the streets. The residents are now coming back to write their names on the map and show where their families used to live.

**A man shows his son where their family once lived at the District Six Museum in Cape Town.**

## Robben Island

Robben Island, South Africa's newest museum, opened on January 1, 1997, and is already its most famous. The museum was once a prison. Nelson Mandela spent eighteen of his twenty-seven years in jail there. Both the tiny cell in which he was confined and the limestone quarry where he broke rocks are now part of the tourist site.

Although there were many ordinary criminals on Robben Island, it was political prisoners like Mandela who made the prison famous. Located just 7 miles (12 km) off the coast of Cape Town, the prison island became known as the University of Robben Island. Younger black activists were jailed with older, better educated political prisoners. After each long day of hard labor, the older generation would pass along their knowledge and experience to the young people.

# New Nation, New Challenges

SOUTH AFRICA HAS ENJOYED A UNIQUE AND LARGELY SUCcessful shift from white minority rule to true democracy. But its long history of apartheid has made it difficult for the nation to overcome some of the challenges it faces—perhaps the most difficult being how to deal with AIDS, unemployment, and crime. These enormous problems are intertwined. All three have to be solved if the people of South Africa can expect a better life.

*Opposite:* **A view of sky-scrapers and other buildings in downtown Cape Town**

## Searching the Skies

In some ways, South Africa is among the most modern nations on Earth. In 2005, it opened a remarkable facility called the Southern African Large Telescope, or SALT. The largest telescope in the Southern Hemisphere, SALT will allow scientists to search the distant skies and research outer space. The site, in the most remote part of the Northern Cape province, was chosen because the air is so clear. There are no lights or air pollution to interfere with the viewing.

AIDS is a disease that afflicts people all around the world. In South Africa, an estimated five million people—most of them married men and women—are infected with HIV, the virus that causes AIDS. If a pregnant woman has the virus, she passes the disease on to her baby. About six hundred people die from AIDS in South Africa every single day. As a result, the average life expectancy there has declined from 66 years to 44 years.

Researchers have discovered medicines that can slow down the disease and help people live with AIDS. In some parts of the world, the epidemic has slowed, but not in South Africa. There are two main reasons for this. The first is the cost of the medicines. At about $100 a month, they are too expensive for the average South African. The second reason is that South Africa's president, Thabo Mbeki, does not believe HIV causes AIDS. He says AIDS is caused by poverty. For a time, his government refused to allow doctors to treat people with the medicines that control

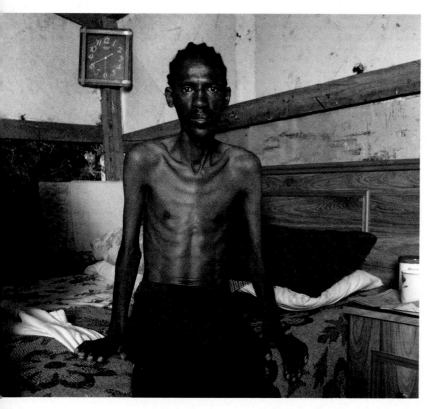

**One of the millions of South Africans suffering from AIDS**

## Fighting AIDS

Zackie Achmat is head of the Treatment Action Campaign (TAC), a group that is working to get HIV-AIDS patients the drugs they need. Achmat has HIV himself, but for many years, he refused to take the drugs he needed until they were available to the majority of South Africans. He even took the government to the Constitutional Court to try to gain access to drugs for his fellow citizens. On November 4, 2004, TAC staged a nationwide protest because the Minister of Health had treated only fifteen thousand people with the drugs, not the fifty thousand they had promised. That number is just a fraction of the people who need treatment.

the disease. He said he didn't know if the drugs were safe. At least half a million South Africans died from the disease during the time the government would not allow the drugs to be used. Although these drugs are now allowed in South Africa, their use is still not widespread.

The huge death toll from AIDS has created a generation of children who are "AIDS orphans." In many cases, both their parents have died from the disease. AIDS is now the main cause of death in women between ages fifteen and thirty-nine, the prime childbearing years.

**Police Officers at Memorial Wall in Johannesburg**

This huge number of AIDS orphans has led to a rise in crime. Without parents or anyone taking care of them, they have no way to support themselves or pay for their school fees. So they turn to crime in order to survive. Whatever they learn, they learn on the street. They don't learn the history of their own people. They don't learn about their cultures. They become "street kids," and their numbers are growing.

### Crime

Crime threatens the everyday lives of people in South Africa. In recent years, violent crime has been increasing. More murders are committed with guns in South Africa than anywhere else in the world. The murder rate there is ten times higher than that in the United States. Most of the murders take place in the poor, crowded townships. In these cases, both the victim and the criminal are black. Crimes against white people are more likely to be theft. Personal attacks, especially violence against women, have made entire neighborhoods extremely dangerous. In some areas, drivers no longer stop for red lights because violent carjackings are so common.

More cars are stolen in Johannesburg than anywhere else in the country. The cars are driven to the Mozambique border where they are sold or stripped down for their parts. Cape Town, which is far from any border, has very little of this type of crime. In Cape Town, burglaries and purse snatchings are much more common. Many people have been the victims of these crimes over and over again.

## Mealie Pap and Boerewors

The foods that white and black people eat represent their different cultures. White people are used to choosing from a wide variety of foods and having something different for each of their meals, day after day.

Poor black people usually have a porridge made from corn flour called mealie pap. This dish is eaten every day by many black South Africans. In the cities, black women can buy corn flour that is already prepared. In the rural areas, they grow their own corn and then pound it into a flour before it can be cooked. Ears of corn are also called mealies. Roasted mealies—corn on the cob—are a favorite food.

South Africans enjoy barbecues just as Americans do. They call them *braais*. The pleasant climate makes it possible to cook outdoors most of the year. A typical braai includes *boerewors*, a sausage made with a variety of meats. The spices that are used are often a family recipe. Afrikaners take great pride in their homemade boerewors.

Another typical South African food is *biltong*. Made of meat that has been dried, biltong is similar to meat jerky but is more delicious. It can be made of any kind of meat, even ostrich, antelope, or crocodile.

In South Africa, there is a growing gap between the rich and the poor. Although most of the rich are white and most of the poor are black, there is an expanding black middle class. Many of them left the country during apartheid and have now returned to their native land. They are better educated than most poor blacks and are able to take advantage of the changes in South Africa.

Most whites in South Africa (and a small number of blacks) live in comfortable homes with clean water and electricity. Many have swimming pools. Whites have cars as well

**Wealthy South Africans dine at Melrose Arch in Johannesburg.**

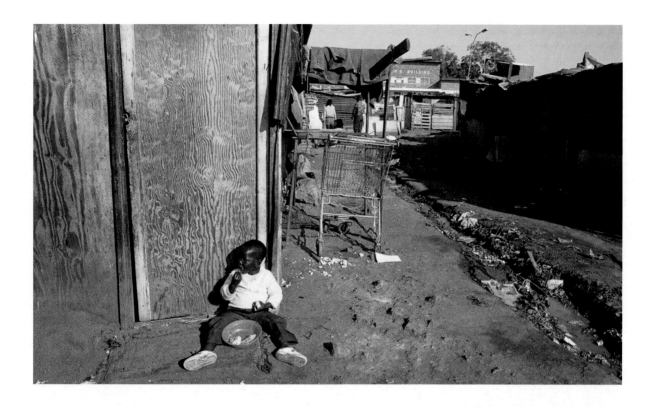

A poor South African child eats outside a shack in Alexandra Township.

as jobs that pay well and that allow them time to enjoy leisure activities. Their children attend schools that have computers, well-furnished classrooms, and enough textbooks for every student. In cities, there is about one doctor for every seven hundred people. But in isolated rural areas, there is only one doctor for every ten thousand to thirty thousand people. This means that most people do not have access to health care.

The vast majority of black South Africans live in poverty, without electricity and clean water. Most of their homes are built out of any materials that can be found. In rural areas, houses may be built of mud and thatch, with wooden poles for support. During apartheid, houses in urban townships were

A slum near Crossroads

built without running water. These were meant to be temporary homes, used only while a black person was working in a "white" city. But for millions of people in these townships, these are the only homes they have ever known. Now the houses are slowly being upgraded, but the job is enormous and very expensive.

South Africa's constitution guarantees its citizens decent housing. The problem is fulfilling that guarantee. A flood of people looking for jobs is overwhelming the cities, especially Johannesburg and Cape Town. Millions of people are one step away from being homeless. They live in shacks that are typically made of metal sheets called zincs. The inside is covered with paper and cardboard. In some areas, the shacks stretch as far as the eye can see. Some communities of shacks are more than twenty years old now. Unable to stop the flow of people, the government has begun paving streets and providing water in these communities.

Slums can spring up quickly. Residents of a wealthy white community in Hout Bay, near Cape Town, woke up one morning to find that a number of shacks had been built just across the valley. Whites and blacks formed a committee and agreed to limit the size of the camp in exchange for electricity and plumbing. The camp is called Mandela Village.

Bridging the gap between rich and poor may be the government's most difficult task. Although South Africa is strong economically, it will take years, perhaps even generations, to create a better standard of living for the millions of people who now live in these shacks.

## Madam and Eve

In South Africa, the difference in lifestyles between rich and poor can be striking. This difference is played out every single day when black maids enter the homes of their white employers. Maids travel from a black township on buses, trains, or taxis. In South Africa, "taxis" are actually minivans. They are meant to hold nine to twelve people, but they are often packed with up to twenty people. It can take a maid two or three such rides to arrive at the employer's home. The white employer usually lives in a pleasant suburb. The maid may not have electricity or hot water at home.

When the maid arrives at work, she passes through a locked gate. A wall around the property encloses a lovely

**Black South African maids sit at a fountain in Johannesburg.**

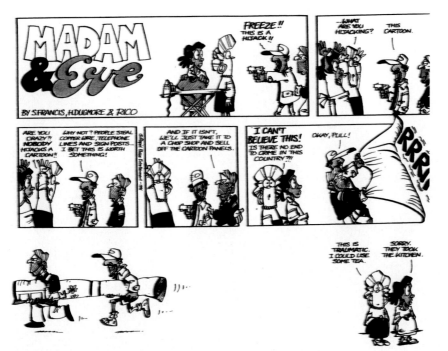

Madam & Eve, a popular South African comic strip

garden, a place for children to play, and, often, a swimming pool. Expensive cars sit in the driveway. The house has all the latest kitchen equipment and several bathrooms.

A clever comic strip called *Madam & Eve* has shown the changes in the relationship between maid and employer since the end of apartheid. In the strip, "Eve," the maid, helps her white employer, "Madam," understand life in the new South Africa. They go through the changes together but from completely different points of view.

One strip captured the impact of crime on the lives of all South Africans. Thieves enter Madam's home and steal the actual comic strip, rolling it up like a carpet and running out of the house. Although humorous, it points out the way crime affects everyone in South Africa.

High school students in
Johannesburg

## Teenage South Africans

The rituals of teenagers' lives depend very much on where they live. In the city, teens go to hip-hop dance parties that last all night. They are very expensive, costing as much as forty rand (about seven dollars) to get in. That's twice as much as it costs to go to a movie there.

Life in the rural areas is totally different for teens. For many boys, this is a time to be initiated, to learn about the rituals of their cultures. At the same time, they are also expected to go to school and learn skills that will be useful in a modern South

Africa. As a result, the time they spend on the ceremony that marks their entry into young adulthood has been shortened. A feast is prepared and the ceremony takes place, with the whole community involved. Boys go away from their families. They spend time with the elders, who teach them about their history and culture. Once a boy has gone through this ceremony, he is considered an adult member of his community.

**Xhosa boys walk alongside a road during a traditional ceremony in Bisho.**

## Wire Toys

Homemade wire toys are popular with children in South Africa. The toys are made by twisting bits of wire into objects with wheels such as a bicycle. The wire extends into a handle that the child uses to push the toy along the ground.

When tourists began buying these wire toys, the people who make them were encouraged to create more complicated pieces. Street vendors now sell wire motorcycles, wire saxophones, and whole wire orchestras.

### Josie's World

Teenagers growing up in South Africa today do not remember apartheid. Their lives are very different from those of their parents. Josephine (Josie) Buarte, a teenager who lives in Pretoria, was born the year Nelson Mandela walked out of prison. Her parents faced restrictions everywhere they went, but Josie sees only possibilities.

**Josie Buarte during computer class**

When her parents bought their house in 1991, because they were black, they had to ask the neighbors' permission to move in. In the past, a talented black teenager like Josie would have had to fight just to go to a decent school. But Josie attends an excellent private school, where she has a challenging list of subjects. It costs her parents 35,000 rand a year ($6,000) to send her there.

Josie lives in Pretoria, an Afrikaans-speaking area, so she is still required to take Afrikaans in school. "I'm finding Afrikaans very difficult," she said. "We don't speak Afrikaans to each other, but sometimes I speak it to my cousin as a joke." The only black teacher in her school was hired to teach Sepedi, the black language that is used in the surrounding area. "They offer Sepedi as a subject, but very few white students take it," she says. Subjects such as math, computer science, drama, history, and music are on her schedule.

"I am an art person," she says. "I like drama, and I take piano lessons three times a week. I like all kinds of music, classic and contemporary. The radio in my room is always on. Nearly everything we watch on TV and what we wear, the foods we eat, is Western." By Western, she means American. "Books, music, TV—it's all Western. You hardly find any local movies. I think South Africa, being a very good country, we have the potential to develop our own movies."

| National Holidays | |
|---|---|
| New Year's Day | January 1 |
| Human Rights Day | March 21 |
| Good Friday | March or April |
| Easter Sunday | March or April |
| Easter Monday | March or April |
| Family Day | March 31 |
| Freedom Day | April 27 |
| Workers' Day | May 1 |
| Youth Day | June 16 |
| National Women's Day | August 9 |
| Heritage Day | September 24 |
| Day of Reconciliation | December 16 |
| Christmas Day | December 25 |
| Day of Goodwill | December 26 |

## Return of the Land

During apartheid, millions of South Africans lost their land. But even before that time, generations of black South Africans had been thrown off their land. Land claims are one of the most difficult issues to solve.

In 1999, a group of San—South Africa's earliest residents— became among the first to get back a piece of their traditional land. Historically, they lived in the Kalahari Desert, now part of the Kalahari Gemsbok National Park. They were given 62,000 acres (25,000 hectares) of land in the southern part of the park, as well as another 100,000 acres (40,000 hectares) of private land next to the park. This is a very dry area, where few people but the San can survive.

Sand dunes and animal tracks in the Kalahari Gemsbok National Park

Land claims are a big financial burden on the South African government. The private land given back to the San was purchased from white farmers for $2.43 million (15 million rand).

## The Future

What does the future hold for South Africa? It is likely to continue on much as it is today. Most of the political power will be in the hands of the black majority. But most of the wealth will remain in the hands of the white minority. The people will continue to struggle with unemployment, AIDS, and crime.

In June 2005, President Mbeki fired the deputy president,

**View of Cape Town from Signal Hill**

Jacob Zuma, who was accused of corruption. The position of deputy president is the second most important in the country, so it was big news when Mbeki named Phumzile Mlambo-Ngcuka, a woman, to this post. Mlambo-Ngcuka had been the minister of minerals and energy. In that position, she demanded that the mining companies, especially the diamond firms, create more jobs in the industry.

Today, millions of South Africans are flocking to the cities looking for work. The government is trying to build houses for them. More people have clean water and sanitation than ever before. More children attend school. Construction cranes dot the skylines, proof that money is flowing into the country. But despite these changes, many adults who did not receive an education under apartheid will not find a role in this growing economy.

South Africa has some of the world's richest people and some of the poorest. Many remain isolated, while others are able to meet people from different races and ethnic groups. South Africa is, and will remain, an unusually complex country.

# Timeline

| South African History | | World History | |
|---|---|---|---|
| The San live in what is now South Africa. | ca. 28,000 B.C. | | |
| | | 2500 B.C. | Egyptians build the Pyramids and the Sphinx in Giza. |
| | | 563 B.C. | The Buddha is born in India. |
| The Khoikhoi arrive in what is now South Africa. | ca. A.D. 100 | | |
| Bantu-speaking Africans migrate into South Africa. | ca. 300 | | |
| | | A.D. 313 | The Roman emperor Constantine recognizes Christianity. |
| | | 610 | The Prophet Muhammad begins preaching a new religion called Islam. |
| | | 1054 | The Eastern (Orthodox) and Western (Roman) Churches break apart. |
| | | 1066 | William the Conqueror defeats the English in the Battle of Hastings. |
| | | 1095 | Pope Urban II proclaims the First Crusade. |
| | | 1215 | King John seals the Magna Carta. |
| | | 1300s | The Renaissance begins in Italy. |
| | | 1347 | The Black Death sweeps through Europe. |
| | | 1453 | Ottoman Turks capture Constantinople, conquering the Byzantine Empire. |
| Portuguese explorer Bartolomeu Dias becomes the first European to reach South Africa. | 1488 | | |
| | | 1492 | Columbus arrives in North America. |
| | | 1500s | The Reformation leads to the birth of Protestantism. |
| Jan van Riebeeck arrives from Holland and establishes the first white settlement in South Africa. | 1652 | | |
| | | 1776 | The Declaration of Independence is signed. |
| | | 1789 | The French Revolution begins. |
| The British take over the Cape Colony from the Dutch. | 1795 | | |
| Shaka becomes the leader of the Zulus. | 1815 | | |
| The Boers begin the Great Trek away from the Cape. | 1835 | | |
| | | 1865 | The American Civil War ends. |

## South African History

| | |
|---|---|
| Diamonds are discovered near present-day Kimberley. | **1867** |
| The Zulus defeat the British at the Battle of Isandlwana. | **1879** |
| Gold is discovered in Johannesburg. | **1886** |
| The Anglo-Boer War is fought. | **1899–1902** |
| The Union of South Africa is created from British colonies and Boer republics. | **1910** |
| The Natives' Land Act is passed, dividing South Africa into "white" areas and "black" areas. | **1913** |
| The National Party wins election and begins establishing apartheid policies. | **1948** |
| Police kill 69 black people at a peaceful protest in Sharpeville; the African National Congress and the Pan Africanist Congress are banned. | **1960** |
| Nelson Mandela is imprisoned. | **1962** |
| On June 16, police fire on student protestors in Soweto, killing 600. | **1976** |
| Nelson Mandela is freed from prison. | **1990** |
| Apartheid is abolished. | **1992** |
| Nelson Mandel and F. W. de Klerk are jointly awarded the Nobel Peace Prize. | **1993** |
| South Africa's first democratic elections are held, and Nelson Mandela is elected president. | **1994** |
| A constitution guaranteeing rights for all becomes law. | **1996** |

## World History

| | |
|---|---|
| **1914** | World War I breaks out. |
| **1917** | The Bolshevik Revolution brings communism to Russia. |
| **1929** | Worldwide economic depression begins. |
| **1939** | World War II begins, following the German invasion of Poland. |
| **1945** | World War II ends. |
| **1957** | The Vietnam War starts. |
| **1969** | Humans land on the moon. |
| **1975** | The Vietnam War ends. |
| **1979** | Soviet Union invades Afghanistan. |
| **1983** | Drought and famine in Africa. |
| **1989** | The Berlin Wall is torn down, as communism crumbles in Eastern Europe. |
| **1991** | Soviet Union breaks into separate states. |
| **1992** | Bill Clinton is elected U.S. president. |
| **2000** | George W. Bush is elected U.S. president. |
| **2001** | Terrorists attack World Trade Towers, New York, and the Pentagon, Washington, D.C. |
| **2003** | The U.S. invades Iraq. |

# Fast Facts

**Official name:** Republic of South Africe

**Capital:** Cape Town (legislative);
Pretoria/Tshwane (administrative);
Bloemfontein (judicial)

Johannesburg

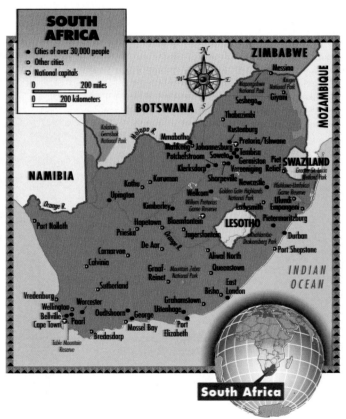

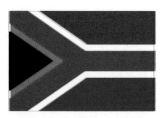

South Africa's flag

Wildflowers in the wilderness

**Official languages:** Sepedi, Sesotho, Setswana, siSwati, Tshivenda, Xitsonga, Afrikaans, English, isiNdebele, isiXhosa, and isiZulu

**Official religion:** None

**National anthem:** "Nkosi Sikelel' iAfrika"
"Lord Bless Africa"

**Government:** Democratic republic

**Head of state and government:** President

**Area:** 472,281 square miles (1,223,201 sq km)

**Bordering countries:** Mozambique and Swaziland in the northeast, Botswana and Zimbabwe in the north, Namibia in the northwest. Lesotho is completely surrounded by South Africa in the center-east.

**Highest elevation:** Mount Injasuti, 11,181 feet (3,408 m)

**Lowest elevation:** Sea level

**Average temperatures:**

|  | July | January |
|---|---|---|
| Cape Town | 54°F (12.2°C) | 70°F (20.9°C) |
| Johannesburg | 51°F (10.4°C) | 58°F (20.1°C) |

**Average annual rainfall:** Varies from more than 40 inches (100 cm) per year in the Drakensbergs and coast of Natal to almost no rain in the northwest.

**National population (2002 est.):** 42,718,530

The Apartheid Museum

Currency

**Population of largest cities (2001):**

| | |
|---|---|
| Johannesburg | 3,225,812 |
| Cape Town | 2,893,215 |
| Durban | 2,117,650 |
| Pretoria/Tshwane | 1,104,479 |
| Port Elizabeth | 749,921 |

**Famous landmarks:**
- ▶ *Nelson Mandela statue*, Johannesburg
- ▶ *Table Mountain*, Cape Town
- ▶ *Robben Island*, Cape Town
- ▶ *Kruger National Park*, Northern Province and Mpumalanga
- ▶ *The Apartheid Museum*, Johannesburg
- ▶ *Sterkfontein Caves*, Krugersdorp

**Industry:** South Africa's economy was built on gold and diamond mining. Mining remains important to the nation. Even today, South Africa is the world's largest producer of gold, chromium, and platinum. But its economy is also more varied. It has a full range of manufacturing companies and the best ports in all of southern Africa. Agriculture accounts for less than 5 percent of South Africa's economic production.

**Currency:** The South African rand is worth about 15 cents in U.S. money. Each rand is divided into 100 cents.

**Weights and measures:** Metric system

**Literacy rate (2003):** 86.4 percent

High school students

Nelson Mandela

**Common words and phrases in isiZulu:**

| | |
|---|---|
| *Sawubona* | a greeting that means good morning, good afternoon, good evening |
| *Yebo* | Yes |
| *Cha* | No |
| *Ngiyabonga* | Thank you |
| *Kunjani?* | How are you? |
| *Mana kancane* | One minute! |

**Famous South Africans:**

Christiaan Barnard (1922–2001)
*Surgeon*

Willie Bester (1956– )
*Artist*

Steve Biko (1946–1977)
*Anti-apartheid activist*

J. M. Coetzee (1940– )
*Novelist who won the Nobel Prize for Literature*

Athol Fugard (1932– )
*Playwright*

Nadine Gordimer (1923– )
*Winner of the Nobel Prize for Literature*

Miriam Makeba (1932– )
*Singer*

Nelson Mandela (1918– )
*Anti-apartheid leader and the first president of democratic South Africa*

Harry Oppenheimer (1908–2000)
*Chairman of De Beers Consolidated Mines*

Shaka (1787–1828)
*Founder of the Zulu nation*

Desmond Tutu (1931– )
*Anglican archbishop and the head of the Truth and Reconciliation Commission*

# To Find Out More

## Books

- Corona, Laurel. *South Africa*. San Diego: Lucent, 2000.

- Gleimius, Nita, Evelina Sibanyoni, and Emma Mthimunye. *The Zulu of Africa*. Minneapolis: Lerner, 2003.

- Green, Jen. *South Africa*. Austin, TX: Raintree/Steck-Vaughn, 2001.

- Green, Robert. *Nelson Mandela: Activist for Equality*. Chanhassen, MN: The Child's World, 2003.

- Rosmarin, Ike, and Dee Rissik. *South Africa*. New York: Benchmark Books, 2003.

## Music

- Ladysmith Black Mambazo. *The Best of Ladysmith Black Mambazo*. Shanachie, 1992.

- Makeba, Miriam. *Mama Africa: The Very Best of Miriam Makeba*. Manteca, 2001.

## Web Sites

▶ **SouthAfrica.info**
http://www.southafrica.info
*For much more about the history,
geography, and people of South Africa.*

▶ **South Africa Government Online**
http://www.gov.za
*The official site of the South African
government offers lots of basic
information, statistics, and speeches.*

▶ **Welcome to South Africa**
http://www.southafrica.net
*The official South African Tourism site
provides a wealth of information about
the nation.*

## Organizations and Embassies

▶ **Embassy of the Republic of
South Africa**
3051 Massachusetts Avenue, NW
Washington, DC 20008
202-232-4400

▶ **Shared Interest
Investing in South Africa's Future**
121 West 27th Street, #905
New York, NY 10001
212-337-8548
http://sharedinterest.org

# Index

Page numbers in *italics* indicate illustrations.

population, 78–79, 83
prehistoric, 30
refugees, 83, 83
San, 18, 31, 33, 34, 36, 77,
    125–126
Sotho, 80
Southern Sotho, 78
Sowetan, 32
Swazi, 79, 80–81
teenagers, 78, 122–123, 122, 124
Tembu, 53
Tsonga, 78
Tswana, 78, 80
Venda, 79
Xhosa, 8, 37, 60, 76, 78, 79–80,
    79, 123
Zulu, 21, 27, 38, 39, 70, 78, 79,
    80, 80, 84, 102, 103
Pietersen, Hector, 48
plant life
    Cape Floral Region, 31
    jacaranda trees, 63
    king protea (national flower),
        25, 25
    Skeleton Coast, 20
    Table Mountain, 19
platinum mining, 64, 65
population, 81, 83
Pretoria, 21, 62–63, 63, 125
Pretorious, Jaco, 98
provinces
    Gauteng, 80
    governments, 59
    KwaZulu-Natal, 27, 29, 33, 70, 78
    Mpumalanga, 80
    National Council of Provinces, 57

Northern Cape, 111, *111*
Western Cape, 68


**R**

radio programs, 103
Rainbow Concert for Peace and
    Democracy, 9
Ramaphosa, Cyril, 67, 67
rand (currency), 72, 72
religion
    African Independent churches, 85
    Anglican Church, 85, 91
    Christianity, 85, 85, 86, 86, 88–89,
        88, 89–90, 91
    Dutch Reformed Church, 86,
        88–89, 88
    Hinduism, 93
    Judaism, 93, 93
    Muslims, 82, 92, 93
    polygamy and, 89
    sangomas (traditional healers),
        87–88, 87, 90
    traditional, 86
    Zion Christian Church, 89–90, 90
reptilian life, 24, 24
reserves, 19, 19, 26–27, 28–29, 69,
    69, 70, 70
rhinoceroses, 27, 27, 69
Rhodes, Cecil, 40, 40
Riebeeck, Jan van, 35, 36, 107
rivers, 16, 39
Robben Island, 19, 31, 31, 109, 109
Robertson Vineyards, 68
rock hyraxes, 19
rugby, 97–98, 98

**S**

San people, 18, 31, 33, 33, 34, 36, 77,
    125–126
sangomas (traditional healers), 87–88,
    87, 90
Schoeman, Roland, 99
Self-Employed Women's Union, 75
Sepedi language, 77, 125
Sesotho language, 77
Setswana language, 77
Shabalala, Joseph, 102
Shaka (Zulu chief), 27, 38
*Shaka Zulu* television series, 70
Shakaland village, 70
Shamwari Private Game Reserve,
    70, 70
Sharpeville township, 46, 56
siSwati language, 77, 80
Skeleton Coast, 20
slavery, 39
soccer, 96, 98–99
Sontonga, Enoch, 60
Sophiatown district, 45
Sotho language, 80
Sotho people, 80
South African Large Telescope
    (SALT), 111, *111*
South African National Gallery, 107
South African Republic, 39
South African Students Organization
    (SASO), 47
South Atlantic Race, 100
Southern Right Whales, 25, 25
Southern Sotho people, 78
Sowetan people, 32
Soweto language, 80

# Meet the Authors

J

ASON LAURÉ has spent the last four years living in South Africa, working on a memoir of his thirty years as a photographer in Africa. During that time, he photographed and observed the dramatic changes taking place in South Africa. He traveled throughout the country, from diamond mines on the west coast to Durban on the east coast. He has seen the positive changes that have taken place since the end of apartheid as well as the problems that have become even more serious. His first visit to South Africa was in 1977, a year after the Soweto uprising.

Ettagale Blauer spent more than a year in South Africa in the last decade, working with Jason Lauré on his memoir and gathering material for this newly revised edition of *South Africa* in the Enchantment of the World series. During her travels, she was delighted with how people of all races mingled while performing the everyday acts of life—shopping, going to the movies, dining in restaurants-in places that were once open only to whites. But she has also been dismayed at the country's rising crime rate and the increasing number of people living in shacks, unable to benefit from South Africa's freedom.

# Photo Credits